# Conduct for the Crayon Crowd

by
Edna Gerstner
(Author of *Idelette, Song by the River,*
and *Jonathan and Sarah*)

**Soli Deo Gloria**
*. . . for instruction in righteousness . . .*

# Soli Deo Gloria Publications

P.O. Box 451, Morgan, PA 15064
(412) 221-1901/FAX 221-1902

\*

\*

ISBN 1-57358-061-9

# Contents

Contents

# Preface for Parents

Before I had a daughter of my own, I did not realize how very full of questions and ethical problems the life of a preschool child could be.

I started to write these stories to meet a need of my own child. As I read the pages to her, I noted her suggestions. When she questioned the meaning of a word, I used a simpler one. When she disliked a story, I discarded it. Finally in my notebook I collected, before she was six, the stories included in this book.

Some incidents really happened; some did not. But all *could* have happened, and are within the possibility range of her preschool mind.

This is my daughter's book. And so I must dedicate it to my stern little critic and co-author, my daughter Rachel.

*Edna Gerstner*

# From the Co-author

When I was little, my mother's stories of India opened a world of mystery and adventure to me. Her vivid descriptions of tigers in the jungle, cobras coiled up under dolls, and lonely walks in the Himalayan mountains captivated me in a manner no television program ever could.

Her stories were all spun from the bedrock of real life, which made them all the more compelling to me. I was learning about my ancestors, their journeys, their faith, and the dreams that took them halfway around the world to lands as far away and exotic as Ali Baba's cave.

It is a heritage I am proud of. Now a storyteller and teacher myself, I credit my mother as a major influence in my choice of careers. Her ability to spin a good tale and to describe the world around her in thoughtful, descriptive prose is a quality I absorbed during the "twilight storytelling hours" contained in this collection.

My mother also has the rare knack of observing the simple stuff of life and elevating it to a profound level. She has the ability to turn a simple incident into a parable of the spirit. Thus her stories of panthers, stray dogs, pythons, and Great Danes take on a rich, spiritual texture to be read and mulled on more than once.

I hope you enjoy my mother's stories, and the conversations we created together as mother and daughter. They reflect some of the most treasured memories of my childhood.

*Rachel (Gerstner) Pruitt*

# What Shall We Call It?

Mother sat down at the typewriter and fed the paper into the machine. Right away Rachel, age four, came and hung over her mother's shoulder. Big sister Judy, thirteen, kept on playing with the baby.

"Are you going to write another chapter in my book, Mother?" asked Rachel.

"Yes, honey. If baby Jonathan doesn't yell too loud. And if big sister can keep him happy. How about sitting near me and helping me? You know we are co-authors."

"What's a co-ther, Mother?"

"It means you are a writer of the book, too. Today I want to decide a very important question. What shall we call our book?"

Rachel drew her dark eyebrows together so Mother knew she was thinking very hard.

"What do you think of calling it *The Book of Baby Ethics*?" offered Mother.

"Oh, Mother!" said Judy, who was listening in. "Nobody Rachel's age would know what you mean by 'ethics.' "

"Do you?" asked Mother.

Judy blushed. "No, I don't. And I'm thirteen!"

"What's another word for that word we don't

know, Mother?" asked Rachel. "A baby word."

"Another word for 'ethics'? How about 'behavior'?"

The children shook their heads. "Too big a word too. It is hard to find a baby word for 'ethics.' You almost need to describe it. I have it! We could call the book *Baby, Be Good*."

"Oh, Mother! I'm not a baby. I don't like that name. Really, I don't like either of those titles because they have the word 'baby' in them. Jonathan's the baby. I'm not."

Mother sighed. "I'm sorry. I keep forgetting how very grown-up you are." And Mother put an arm about her co-author.

"Why not call it *Toddler Talks*?" suggested big sister.

"A toddler?" Rachel was cross. "I'm not a toddler. I can walk every bit as well as you, Sister Judy!"

"Now what was it," Mother asked, "that the newspaper advertisement called you when it showed those pretty dresses for a girl your age?"

"The Crayon Set," answered Rachel.

"Since 'conduct' is about the babiest word I can think of that means 'ethics,' and if it is too hard maybe the mothers and daddies can explain it to their children, why not call the book *Conduct for the Crayon Set*?"

"Why not make every word begin with the letter 'C' and call it *Conduct for the Crayon Crowd* instead?" suggested Judy.

"*Conduct for the Crayon Crowd*. I like that," said Mother. "How about you, Rachel, my co-author?"

"Well, I'm not sure."

"We're having a harder time naming our book than when we named the baby! We do want everybody to be happy," said Mother, sounding tired.

"Who's not happy?" said Daddy, coming in the door.

"Daddy!" squealed Rachel. And Daddy was surrounded by a flutter of skirts and tiny arms. "We have a problem."

"Tell me about it," said Daddy.

"What shall we name the new book Mommy and I are writing?"

"What is the book about?"

"It tells children who are grown-up—but not grown-up enough for school—to be good."

"Now let me see. How does this sound? Why not call the book *Life Begins at Four*?"

Mother laughed, but nobody else did.

"I have decided," said Rachel. "We will call it *Conduct for the Crayon Crowd*."

"Rachel, Rachel, quite contrary, how does your little book grow?" teased Daddy.

"It's almost finished. You don't mind my not

choosing your name, do you, Daddy?"

"Not at all. It's your book."

"Type it, type it now, Mother. Type the name!" said Rachel.

And so Mother wrote in capitals on the blank sheet of paper: *Conduct for the Crayon Crowd.*

"It looks pretty," said the co-author.

And so the book was named.

# Be Like Jesus

"Looking unto Jesus." Hebrews 12:2

Whenever anybody asked Rachel what she wanted to be when she grew up, she always said, "I want to be a sissy."

"It was wonderful," thought Rachel, "to have a big sister like Judy." Some day she wanted to be just like her. It was a very happy day for her when Mommy told her that she was going to become a big sissy. She remembered how she could hardly wait for the time to come for Mother to go to the hospital and come home with a baby brother or sister. How she longed for that day when she would really and truly herself be a big sissy.

She took her job very seriously. At first she was a good big sissy by bringing Mommy diapers, or the many, many things little babies seemed to be always needing. Or she would be a good sissy by very gently rocking the cradle when the baby cried. And now that the baby was six months old she was a good sissy by bringing him toys or playing peek-a-boo with him. Everybody would say that some day she would get tired of being a big sissy, but she never did.

Mother smiled one day as she watched Rachel

playing gently with her baby brother. "Look at his eyes when he looks up at you," she said. "He loves you very much. He loves you just as much already as you love your big sister, Judy. Do you know, Rachel, if he could talk, if I asked him what he wanted to be when he grows up, do you know what I think he would say?"

Rachel did not answer. She smiled. She thought she knew what Mommy was going to say. But it was fun sometimes to hear her say it anyway.

"What would he say, Mommy?"

" 'I want to be a sissy!' "

Mommy! He's a little boy. He couldn't be a sissy!"

Mommy laughed. "You caught me that time. But I'm sure, since you are so good to him, he would want to grow up and be just like you. Do you know there is someone who is always kind, patient, and understanding of us? There is someone that we all want to be like. Can you guess who I mean?"

"Yes, Mommy," said Rachel. "Jesus."

"He is our elder brother, our big brother. And we do want to be just like Jesus. How does that song go?"

Rachel sang along with her mother:

*Be like Jesus, this my song,*
*In the home and in the throng;*
*Be like Jesus, all day long!*
*I would be like Jesus.*

"Listen to our gurgler baby, Mommy. He is singing too!"

# Be the Best Little Somebody

"Well done, thou good and faithful servant." Matthew 25:21

"Mommy, I've written a poem for Sunny! Listen!" Rachel came to her mother in the kitchen with a piece of paper in her hands. She had written several letters of the alphabet that she knew on the page.

Mother looked at the letters; then she handed the page back to her daughter. "How about reading it to me?"

"I love you. Coo," Rachel said. "That rhymes, doesn't it?" Her voice was worried.

"It does, and it is beautiful. Come, let me give you a kiss for that."

Rachel came close to her mother to get her kiss. Mother always kissed her on the top of her head when she was especially pleased with her.

"Maybe, someday, you will grow up to be a famous poet. And baby brother will be so proud you wrote your first poem about him. You know, dear, God wants us to use our talents."

"What's a talent, Mommy?"

"A talent is a gift God gives us. It is not something we can touch or see. It is something we can do. He may give one child the gift of song. To another he may give the talent for painting. Perhaps he has given you a gift for writing. He wants us to use these talents for Him.

"Let me tell you a story I have heard Daddy tell in one of his sermons. A Methodist bishop was preaching to a number of men who were going to be ministers. He asked them the question, 'Who is willing to be a nobody for Christ?' One by one all gave the same answer, 'I am.' They thought they were giving the right answer, the one he wanted. But the bishop was not happy. He said very sternly to them, 'Jesus does not want anyone to be a nobody for Him. He wants you to be a somebody for *Him*.'"

"Mommy, do you have time to play the rhyming game with me?"

"Yes, I will be able to as soon as I put this cake into the oven. Now," asked Mother, "what rhymes with joy?"

"Boy!" said Rachel. "It's my turn, and I'll think of a hard one. What rhymes with blue?"

"Let me see—"

"I know, Mommy. New!"

"Well, what do you know?" smiled mother. "Do you know, Rachel, I believe we could mix up all our rhyming words and come up with a poem. Let's bake a poem while we bake our cake. How's this?

What a joy
Is our boy.
He wears blue.
He's brand ...

". . . now you finish it."

"New!" shouted Rachel.

"Good!" said Mommy. "You know, doll, you have always liked to play with words. When you were only three I was towelling you after a hot bath, and the bathroom was cold. I asked you if you were chilly, and do you know what you came up with?"

Rachel knew. This was one of her favorite when-I-was-little stories, but she said, "You tell me again, Mother."

"You said, 'I'm as cold as a bird that forgot to fly South.'"

"And now, my little poet, how about using another talent of yours, and help me frost the cake."

"I'd love to, Mommy," said Rachel. "And may I lick the dish?"

"You may. You are very good at that!"

# Jesus Understands

"They shall call His name Emmanuel . . . God with us."
Matthew 1:23

"Mommy, please make me an apron."

"An apron?" Mother sounded surprised. "Why do you want an apron, dear?"

"Gretel has an apron."

"Oh!" said Mother. She understood. That was the nice thing about mothers. You did not need to explain every little thing to them. Rachel's mother knew that all the last month she had been Dorothy, like Dorothy in *The Wizard of Oz*. This month her favorite book person was Gretel in *Hansel and Gretel*, and so she was Gretel.

"May I watch you while you sew?"

"Yes, if you promise to sit quietly on your chair and not get your fingers near the sewing machine."

Rachel went to her playroom and came back with a chair just her size, sat down, and watched the apron being made.

"When I was a little girl I used to wear a pinafore," Mother said.

"What is a pinafore, Mommy?"

"It's an apron that covers the top as well as the bottom. When we wore pinafores our dresses were

11

always kept clean. When company would come, our mothers would take off our pinafores and we would be sweet and tidy and fit to be seen."

"Did you get dirty, too, Mommy, when you were a little girl?"

"Every bit as dirty as you. Yes, once upon a time, Mommy was a little girl—just like you, with all your problems. And I'll tell you a secret. I wanted my mommy to make me a pinafore because Alice in Wonderland wore a pinafore and she was my favorite person."

"I'm glad you were once a little girl, Mommy. I'm glad you were once just like me."

"And do you know what I am glad about, Rachel? It is that Jesus came down from heaven and was born a baby, and grew up on earth. He could, you know, have come to earth as a grown-up. He knows just how you feel. And he was once a baby, so He knows how Sunny feels." Mother waited. She knew there would be more from Rachel.

"And He was once thirteen, so He knows how Sissy feels. And how old are you, Mommy?"

Mommy smiled, "Let's just say He understands me, too. There! Your apron is done." Mommy tied it around Rachel's waist. "Goodbye, Gretel."

"Goodbye, and thank you, Mommy," said Rachel.

# The Five O'Clock Hour

"A soft answer turneth away wrath; but grievous
words stir up anger." Proverbs 15:1

"I hate meat!" said Rachel, pushing away her
plate.

Mother turned from the oven and said firmly,
"Remember, young lady, this is the five o'clock
hour. Don't try my patience."

"What do you mean by the five o'clock hour?"
asked Judy.

"I was reading an article in the newspaper this
morning, and I was telling Rachel about it. It seems
that about five o'clock each evening in every home
in our country tempers are most tried, more
children get spanked, and more quarrels begin. You
see, every mother has had a long day. Around five,
in our family, Daddy comes home from a full day's
work. You, Judy, have had a big day at school.
Rachel has been playing hard and helping me, and
she is weary. Even our cheerful baby, our little ray
of sunshine, is cranky about five. He can hardly
wait to be put to bed for his long night's sleep. And
so each of us must try especially not to test each
other's patience at this time.

"You, Rachel, if you don't like your meat, what

13

could you say to make Mommy feel better?"

"I don't know."

"Judy, what do you think she could say?"

"She could keep her mouth shut and eat what's on her plate!"

"She could do that. At least that wouldn't make me cross. But how could she make me happy at the five o'clock hour?"

"Maybe I would like the dessert," said Rachel.

"That's right, darling. And you could say nothing about the meat. I don't want you ever to lie to make me happy. But when it came time for the dessert you could say something very nice about it.

"When you first started to talk, Rachel, your very first sentence was, 'Good meal, Mommy.' I remember when you said it. It had been a long day; it was the five o'clock hour, and I was tired. You brightened me up. It made the whole day worthwhile. The Bible has a verse, 'A soft answer turneth away wrath; but grievous words stir up anger.' "

"What is for dessert tonight, Mommy?"

"Ice cream."

"I love ice cream!" said Rachel.

"You see. I feel better already!" said Mother.

"Was I giving a soft answer?" asked Rachel.

"Yes. When you said, 'I hate meat,' those were

grievous words. Now you have turned away wrath, and I am sure we will all enjoy our dinner."

"Here comes Daddy's car. May I let him in?"

"Yes. You may be excused from the table."

"He's late, isn't he?"

"Yes. But remember, no grievous words. Daddy is tired, and it would make him unhappy if you met him at the door with the words, 'You're late!' Can you think of some soft words to say?"

"I could tell him how glad I am he is home."

"That will be fine. He will explain to us why he is late. He always has a good reason. And your words will make him feel happy to be home."

"You'd better hurry! I hear his key in the lock," said Judy.

Rachel pushed in her chair, and ran to the door. Judy exchanged a smile with Mother.

# Family Devotions

"Behold, the Lion of the tribe of Judah." Revelation 5:5

Whenever anyone in the family said the word "devotions," baby Jonathan, who could not talk yet, would understand. He would jump up and down and thump midway between his chest and his stomach. And the family would know what he meant and would sing baby's favorite chorus: "I have the joy, joy, joy, joy, down in my heart."

After baby's favorite motion song, with mother sitting at the piano, the others would gather around and call out their favorite psalms and hymns. When it was Rachel's turn everybody knew the selection would be number 333. For Rachel never tired of singing "Dare to be a Daniel." And when people would ask her why that was her favorite hymn, she would always answer, "I am very fond of kindly lions." And she was. One year she even wanted Santa Claus to bring her a lion for Christmas.

Mother wrote a poem about it for her and called it "Lines for a Lion." It wasn't good poetry, but it made Rachel happy to have a poem that was about her and was her very own. After Mommy read it to her a few times she knew it by heart. You could hear her reciting it to her dolls several times a day.

## "Lines for a Lion"
### by Rachel's Mommy

Dear Santa, send a lion,
Please, one from Daniel's den.
Their picture's in my scrapbook,
And I'm very fond of them.

If you can't spare me Daniel's,
My second choice would be
From Oz, the Cowardly Lion
Who walked with Dorothy.

A favorite book of Rachel's was *The Lion, the Witch and the Wardrobe* by C. S. Lewis. For several months she called herself Lucy after one of the little girls in the book. How she loved to read about the kindly lion. Daddy explained to her that one of the descriptions of Christ was as "Lion of Judah," and that the lion in the book was Jesus.

One Christmas Daddy gave her a picture of a curly-headed child leading a group of wild animals. The little girl's hand was resting on the mane of the lion.

Daddy explained the picture to her. "How sad," he said, "that now we can't walk safely through the jungles, or even pet strange dogs in the city streets. For even animals are not always good. When Adam

sinned all creation fell. "But someday," read
Daddy from Isaiah 11:6–9, " 'the wolf also shall
dwell with the lamb, and the leopard shall lie down
with the kid; and the calf and the young lion and
the fatling together; and a little child shall lead
them. . . . And the lion shall eat straw like the ox.
And the sucking child shall play on the hole of the
asp. . . . They shall not hurt nor destroy in all My
holy mountain.'

"In heaven, my dear, you will not need to ask if
any animal is kind or unkind, or whether you may
pet it or not. You may enjoy, love, and cuddle all
the animals that God has made.

"Tonight, for devotions, we will read together
Rachel's favorite story of Daniel in the lions' den.
What lesson do we learn from it, Judy?"

"You have told us, Daddy, that it is not so much
'dare to be a Daniel,' but do we dare *not* to be a
Daniel."

"And what does that mean?"

"We should be more afraid of an angry God
than of a den of wild beasts. We do not dare
disobey Him."

"Now I shall read. And then we will close by
singing . . ."

"Number 333," finished Rachel.

# Be Content

"Be content with such things as ye have." Hebrews 13:5

Rachel lay on her tummy in her small swimming pool on the porch and kicked and splashed. Near her, in his own little pool, just big enough to hold his little plump body, Sunny made his own effort to soak mommy who was sitting between the pools trying to read.

When drying time came, Mommy first of all pulled out baby brother, and he cooed and gooed and giggled as he was dried.

Then it was Rachel's turn. She loved to be rubbed and wrapped up in the big towel, so big it covered her like a tent. As mother was toweling her long hair, Rachel noticed it hanging down in her face. It was soaking wet and dark in color. "Oh, Mommy, look, look! My hair is black!"

Mother rubbed the wet hair with her towel.

"Oh, please, Mother, make it stay black! Please make it stay black!"

"Why, darling? Don't you like your pretty blonde hair?"

"I want it to be black for your sake. I have heard you say you always wanted a black-haired girl."

"I don't want you changed—not one bit,

darling. You must have heard Mommy teasing. It isn't always easy for little girls to understand. What you have heard me say, no doubt, is that before you were born I had wanted a black-haired boy. And I got just what I wanted, a blonde girl! That means, darling, that often in life we don't get what we think we wanted; but we are very happy with what God sends. There is a verse in the Bible, Philippians 4:11: 'I have learned, in whatsoever state I am, therewith to be content.'

"Do you remember how, before Sunny was born, you and big sister both wanted a girl? But when I brought our little boy back from the hospital you were very happy for him. I remember one lady asked you if you would give the baby to her, and you started to cry. You were very upset."

"She was just teasing, wasn't she?"

"Yes. Grown-ups love to tease. And little girls must try to understand. They should ask questions if they don't.

"Your Aunt Peggy was telling me about a little girl, just about your age, who did not understand something a grown-up said. It was too bad she did not ask about it. It is a sad story. This little girl, too, had a baby brother. He was born with a sick heart. They had to take the baby to Baltimore to the hospital for an operation. The operation did not help the heart and the little baby died. When the mommy came home she felt so badly about it she did not want to talk about the baby brother. And so when the little girl asked about her brother, she said, 'I am sorry, honey, but we lost your baby brother.' For months the little girl hardly spoke to her mother. She was very cross. Do you know why? Do you know what she thought?"

"They had left him somewhere?"

"That is exactly what she thought. How could her mother have been so careless as to lose her precious baby brother? When she learned the truth, she forgave her mother. She understood. She was happy again."

Mother rubbed the golden hair until it shone. "And so, Rachel, when I talk about wanting a black-haired girl, I am teasing. Look how pretty and golden your hair is."

"And you do like it, Mother?"

"I do, dear, just the way it is. And are you glad you have a baby brother?"

"Oh, yes, Mother. I got just what I wanted, too."

# Be Logical

"Thou shalt love the Lord thy God with all thy heart, and with all thy soul, and with all thy mind." Matthew 22:37

It was Daddy's day to baby-sit. At first Rachel did not like the idea of Mommy and Judy going out and not taking her.

"It is good for Mommy to get away from home," said Daddy. "You know Mommy isn't just Mommy. She is a person. She is also Edna."

"I know," said Rachel. "Yesterday I called 'Mommy! Mommy!' I even pulled her skirt. She did not answer me. When I called 'Edna' she jumped. She heard me."

Daddy laughed. "Today while Mommy is being Edna you will have to help me. I am the big baby-sitter and you are my assistant."

"Sunny is wet," said Rachel.

"He is always wet," said Daddy. "How often does Mommy change him?"

"Whenever he gets wet."

"How does she know from a distance?" asked Daddy, who hated to take what he called "unnecessary steps."

"He cries," said Rachel. "He is crying now."

Daddy hated to leave his comfortable armchair.

But duty is duty, so he changed Sunny's diaper. It took a few minutes because the baby seemed to be all legs. Before he could settle in his comfortable armchair Rachel told him it was time for baby's supper, that he ate from tiny baby food jars, and that his favorite meal was plums and farina.

When Daddy went to the kitchen to find this jar he heard Rachel call out, "If you are logical, while you are there, you will also bring the milk."

Daddy laughed. It was a funny word for a little girl to use. But "logic" was one of Rachel's favorite words. It was because she was a very logical little girl that Daddy called her his little logician.

If Daddy said, for example, "If you go outdoors without your coat again you will get spanked," Rachel would always reply, "If I don't go outdoors without my coat I won't get spanked."

After Sunny had been fed and tucked into his cradle, Daddy rocked it with his foot. In this way Daddy, who always tried to do two things at once, had a lap and arms ready for his little logician.

They had their evening Bible reading together. Daddy read Matthew 22:37: "Thou shalt love the Lord thy God with all thy heart, and with all thy soul, and with all thy mind."

"Do you know what loving God with your mind means, Rachel?"

"God wants me to be logical."

Daddy cradled Rachel in his arms. Sunny was already asleep with one fat leg hanging over the edge of the cradle. Daddy gently lifted it and put it back in the cradle and tucked the blue blanket around the baby. "He is getting too big for his cradle. But he hates the crib."

"I do, too," said Rachel. "In the crib Sunny looks like he's in a zoo behind bars. Please let him stay in his pretty blue cradle."

"We shall certainly leave him there tonight. But that cradle is what I would call filled to capacity."

Rachel laughed. Daddy used such big words, but she could guess that if Sunny filled his cradle to capacity it meant he was spilling over the edges.

Rachel loved to be held in her daddy's strong arms. They sat together and rocked without saying a word. It was good to share stillness with Daddy. It was Daddy who finally broke the silence.

He stroked her long, soft, brown hair and said, "You have a fine brain, Rachel."

It made Rachel very happy for Daddy to say that. Other people said she was pretty with her big almond-shaped eyes. Mommy said she was kind. But when Daddy said she had a fine brain, Rachel knew that was the nicest thing Daddy could say to her.

"Remember, sweetheart," said Daddy, "Love God with all your mind."

# Bothering God

"Suffer little children, and forbid them not,
to come unto Me." Matthew 19:14

"Mommy, what is Tippy's big name?"

"Mother smiled. "It is a long one, isn't it? That is why we have made it shorter. Her real name is Xanthippe."

"Xanthippe." Rachel loved to roll her tongue around big words. "Tell me again why we call her Xanthippe."

Rachel loved to hear her favorite stories told over and over again, especially when it was a private family story.

"Once upon a time, before you were born, my darling, a good friend of ours, a little neighbor boy, had a cat he loved. She had five baby kittens. He wanted to give each of them to someone who would love the babies as much as he loved the mother cat. He chose us because he knew we would love the little gray kitten as he wanted her to be loved. That is how Xanthippe became a part of our family. We did love her and she loved us. Instead of us owning her, we soon began to see that she felt she owned us. We were her pets. She soon tried to become the boss of the family.

"Daddy had one habit she did not like. He would sit at his big study desk and open a book to read. She knew that when he put his head in a book he forgot all about her. She was jealous. So whenever he sat down to study, from wherever she was, she would come running and she would sit on his book. She would roll over and purr and be oh so sweet. She would never let him turn a page.

"So Daddy named the kitten Xanthippe, for long, long ago there was a very wise man whose name was Socrates, and he was often bothered— not by a little kitten—but by a wife. She was the first Xanthippe."

"Has Daddy changed? Does he like to have Tippy bother him now?" asked Rachel.

"Sometimes. In fact, most of the time he thinks it is cute. But every once in a while you will hear him say, 'Shoo, Xanthippe. Don't bother me!' "

Rachel wrinkled her eyes into slits and giggled. "He says that to me sometimes too."

Mother smiled. "I'll tell you a secret, kitten. Once in a while he says that to me also. Do you know why he says, 'Please don't bother me'?"

"He has to study his sermon for Sunday."

"Wouldn't we feel terrible if next Sunday he stood in the pulpit and didn't have a sermon to preach. We would know either you or I or Judy or Xanthippe had bothered him. There are times when Daddy must not be bothered. You see, he can't do two things at once."

"Can anybody do two things at once?" asked Rachel.

"Yes," said Mother. "There is someone I know, and you know Him too. Guess who."

Rachel brought her eyebrows together. The inside edges met over her nose. She looked just like her daddy when she tried to think.

"I know, Mommy, I know. God. God can do anything."

"Go to the head of the class," said Mother. "That is why God is never bothered by us. He wants us always to bother Him. We can go to Him always. He is everywhere. He can hear everybody at the same time because He is God. He can do everything at once."

"God will never push me off His lap," said Rachel.

"I like the way you put it."

# Don't Diet

"Blessed are they which do hunger and thirst after righteousness, for they shall be filled." Matthew 5:6

Mother stood looking at herself in a full-length mirror. "I shall have to start dieting tomorrow."

Judy remembered how Mother had looked before Sunny had been born. "You should lose a few pounds," she said.

Rachel started to cry. She threw her arms about her mother's plump waist. "Don't, Mother, don't diet. I don't want to lose a pound of you!"

Judy and Mother both laughed. Rachel never wanted to lose any part of herself. When Mother combed her long hair Rachel would ask, "Are you sure it's rooted?" because her doll Betty Nancy's hair would lift off her scalp if someone combed too hard.

It wasn't that Rachel wasn't brave. Just yesterday she had tripped and fallen hard on the cement sidewalk. Instead of crying she had jumped up and run to comfort her mother, saying, "I'm all right. See, I'm like Betty Nancy. I didn't break. I'm made of rubber."

But she did not want to get even an inch of her hair cut off. It was as if she were losing a piece of her very person with each snip of the scissors. It was as if she were losing a part of her soul.

Mother tried to explain that the body was not a glove with the soul poured into it. One could lose a thumb and still not lose one drop of soul. But Rachel thought like the cannibals. Daddy had explained that the reason why they ate people was that they thought by doing so they could fatten their souls and their tummies—that by eating brave men they could become brave.

"How do we feed our souls, Rachel?"

"We read the Bible; we pray," suggested Judy.

"We go to Sunday school and church," offered Rachel.

"One of the Beatitudes is 'Blessed are they which do hunger and thirst after righteousness.' Which is more important, the soul or the body?"

Neither girl answered. "Many people act as if the body were. They spend all their time and money on it. There is nothing wrong with caring for our bodies. We should bathe, brush our teeth, comb our hair, eat our spinach. But at best these bodies, with all the care in the world, won't last more than a hundred years. But our souls will go on and on and on for ever. How silly to starve our souls."

"But Mommy, what if we stuff our souls and they get too fat for our bodies?"

"You are still thinking like a cannibal, Rachel. You are thinking our bodies are like Sunny's balloon. If we blow it too full of soul, you imagine, the balloon will burst. But we can never get too much food for the soul. You can stuff your soul full of goodies and never have to worry about feeding it too much."

Mommy sighed, passing up a piece of chocolate cake. "How nice that my *soul*, at least, need never go on a diet!"

# Add Love

"And if I have not love, it profiteth me nothing."
1 Corinthians 13:3

Part of the fun of having a daddy who was a preacher, Rachel thought, was that he preached in California. When Daddy preached away from home, sometimes all the family went. Xanthippe was a traveling cat. It was easy with Tippy. She did not take up very much space. But now things were different. Daddy had given the family a Great Dane for Christmas. The trouble with Hamlet, the Dane, was that he thought he was a cat. He had been trained by Tippy, and he had very good cat manners, but he was a dog—the biggest of all dogs. So he and we had problems.

He sat by the door when he wanted to go out instead of barking like a regular dog. He even seemed to purr. Rachel called it "mumpfing." He turned on his inside motor and "mumpfed" when he was happy. When he went to bed on the floor, like Tippy, he would whale around in circles and finally all at once he would fall down, like London Bridge. When Tippy did this nothing happened, but when Hamlet let himself down the very walls would shake and the dishes would rattle in the cupboard. But a trouble even bigger than this was that he liked to curl up in people's lap like a kitten. The moment someone sat down he would come over and at least a part of him, the heaviest part, would settle on that person's lap. When the family went on trips Hamlet always sat on somebody's lap. Everybody loved him for the first mile. After that Hamlet would be passed around from one lap to another. This time Daddy planned a long trip and he remembered that he had said the last time Hamlet had been a passenger, "Never again." Since Daddy was going to California he announced firmly, "Hamlet must stay home."

"I don't want to go if Hamlet can't go," Rachel said, equally as firm.

"Then we will have to stay," said Mother.

"But I don't want to. I want to go with Daddy."

"You can't have it both ways," said Daddy. "You will have to make a decision."

"What is a decision?" asked Rachel.

"It means," said Judy, who always patiently answered these questions of her little sister, "you have to do one thing or the other. You can't do both. If we decide to go, maybe we can find a nice place to leave Hamlet. "

"Let your fingers do the walking through the yellow pages," chanted Rachel, who was the family member who listened to all the commercials on

TV. She ran and brought back the heavy telephone book. The girls sat on either side of Sunny and looked at the advertisements. Sunny thought this was great fun and tried to eat the yellow pages. Mother got him a book of his own to chew up. She sat and knitted while Judy read aloud from the dog boarding ads.

"I don't want Hamlet boarded up," cried Rachel.

"'Boarded' means given a home and fed," explained Judy. "Here's one. The Country Club for Dogs—air conditioned kennels."

Rachel liked the picture with the ad. It was of a dog that looked like Hamlet. He wore glasses and was stretched out under a beach umbrella.

"Let's check that one," said Rachel.

All the other advertisements read, "Dogs Boarded," with no pictures. Finally they found one other ad tucked away almost at the very end. It said simply "Doggy Motel."

"Oh, Hamlet loves motels," said Rachel.

The family all loved motels. When Hamlet went with them he was always on his best behavior. He never dirtied the wall-to-wall carpeting. He never barked. It was a point of honor with the family that even when Hamlet did not go with them they never stayed in any motel where dogs were not welcome.

Mother tried to explain to the children that a

barking dog could be a nuisance. She could understand motels refusing to take people with dogs.

"If Hamlet ever opened his mouth, he would
meow," said Rachel.

"But not all dogs were brought up by mother
cats." But Mother was outvoted. Even when Hamlet was not with them they always chose a "Dogs
Allowed" motel. Rachel would go to the desk to
register with her daddy and would ask, "Do you
take dogs?"

"What kind of dog do you have?" the motel
manager would often ask.

"Our dog is not with us on this trip," Daddy
would answer.

"Do you take dogs?" Rachel would ask again.

Rather puzzled, the manager would answer. If
he said, "No," Rachel would tug on her daddy's
coat and out they would go.

The idea of a motel for dogs pleased Rachel.
"Put two checks by that one," she said.

That night they told Daddy of their two choices.

"We will have to make a decision," said Daddy.
"Let us visit the two places you have checked."

The Country Club for Dogs was very beautiful.
It was a large building surrounded by old trees and
green grass. The owner said with pride that he had
space for two hundred dogs. Rachel kept tugging at
Daddy's coat tails while the men talked together.

Daddy said he would let the man know what the family decided. When they got into the car so that they could speak privately Rachel started to cry.

Daddy tried to reassure her. "What a beautiful place to stay. The man seems to have a very good business. He knows all about dogs."

Rachel cried louder and louder. The family waited until Rachel had used up her tears and was able to talk. "He doesn't love all the dogs, Daddy."

"How can you tell?" Mother asked. "Besides it is very difficult, when you have two hundred dogs, to love each and every one of them."

"Didn't you hear the dog crying?" asked Rachel.

"I heard several dogs howling," said Mother. "But it's like a baby in church. One cries and they all join in. Only one dog may be unhappy. The others may just be barking out of politeness. One dog cries because he is sad, and the other 199 howl to keep him company."

"But didn't you hear what the man said?" asked Rachel.

"He said he would be glad when that howling dog left. He upset the others," said Judy.

"But what if that one dog were Hamlet? You know how lonesome Hamlet gets. And when he is lonesome, you know how loud he gets. Mother says you can hear him for miles. Please, please don't leave him there. I don't want that man to keep Hamlet."

It was a long speech for a little girl. Daddy sighed. "Well, let's visit this other one you have checked."

This time the kennel was located in the country. "Where is the Doggy Motel? I can't see one," said Judy.

A lady came out of a farm home and met them in the driveway. She was young, pretty, with curly hair and a very nice smile. She looked at Rachel whose face was smudged by tears.

"You don't want to leave your dog, do you? I know just how you feel. That is why I opened this motel for dogs. I keep the dogs in the house with me. This is the Doggy Motel." She pointed to the white farm house. "I love dogs. I try to keep them happy when their families are away. Your dog will be lonesome, but I will do my best to comfort him. You can bring his blanket and his favorite toy with him."

"Love him, please, just love him. He is used to so much loving," begged Rachel.

"If you want to leave him with me I will," said the lady.

It did not take the family long to decide which motel was the right one for Hamlet. Daddy took a vote, and all hands went up for the Doggy Motel.

"We will bring him tomorrow," said Daddy. On

the way home he said to his family, "We all chose
the Doggy Motel. Yet both places charge the same
amount. The first one is more efficient. The second is haphazard."

"What is 'haphazard'?" asked Rachel, who
never wanted a big word to escape her.

Judy said, "It means you don't do everything the
same way all the time."

Rachel heaved a sigh of relief.

"She will feed him every day," said Mother,
"but maybe not always at 6:00 p.m. sharp. But then
Hamlet is used to that. He sometimes has to drag
his dish over to me and rattle it to show me it is
empty and that he is hungry."

"I though 'haphazard' meant something terrible," said Rachel. "Now I know that Hamlet will
be happy there. He is a haphazard dog."

"She may not feed him on schedule," said
Mother, "but she will feed him."

"And she will do what the dog-food people say:
'All you add is love,' " said Rachel with a satisfied
smile.

"Which reminds me," said Daddy, "of a Bible
verse for us all to remember. If I give all my pos-
sessions to feed the poor . . . but do not have love,
it profits me nothing."

"We chose well. We chose a landlady for
Hamlet who knows love is the most important in-

gredient in business," said Mother.
    "For dogs and people," said Judy.
    "For Hamlet," said Rachel.

# On Being Adopted

"Ye have received the Spirit of adoption, whereby
we cry, 'Father.' " Romans 8:15

"Are you going to bake a cake for Judy's bird-
day?" asked Rachel.

"Birthday," corrected Mommy.

"Oh, I thought it was 'bird-day' because we sing
like the birds on people's bird-days."

"No, Rachel. The word is 'birth.' It's a new
word for you."

"Let's learn it, Mommy."

"While you help me bake the cake we'll learn
it."

Rachel loved to sift flour. Mother tried not to
say anything when the kitchen floor and Mother's
little helper turned into a snowman in a snow-
storm. While she measured the milk she held the
empty cup for Rachel to see. "There is nothing in
the cup now. It is empty. Now you watch and stop
Mommy when she pours milk until it reaches this
line."

Rachel put her chin on the table and watched.
"Chop, Mommy!" she called. Rachel said most of
her letters plainly, but "s" was a letter she always
pronounced "ch." Mommy knew that when she

said "chop," she meant "stop."

"A birth is something like the milk we poured into this glass. First of all there was no milk. Now the cup is full of milk. Once upon a time there was no Rachel. Then there was a Rachel. Make believe that cup is the world, and Rachel is the milk. The day you came into the world was your birthday."

"Sunny had his birthday in the hospital. I couldn't be there."

"Yes, that's right. You remember a day when there was no Sunny. But when I came back from the hospital there was Sunny. You missed his birthday because Sunny and I stayed in the hospital together for five days after his birthday. But next birthday you will most certainly be there. And you can blow out his one candle."

"I had four candles for my birthday," said Rachel.

"One for each year," said Mommy.

"Why does Judy have two birthdays each year?" asked Rachel.

"That is because Judy is adopted," said Mother. "You see, even Mommy wasn't there for Judy's birthday. She came to live with us when she was eight. So we thought it would be nice if we cele-brated her family birthday with us on the very day when she appeared here. On January 24 we did not have Judy. On January 25 we had a pretty eight-year-old black-haired daughter."

"Which of Judy's bird—birthdays is this?"

"This is her second birthday," said Mommy.

"I wish I could have two birthdays."

"Well, in a way you do. All people who love Jesus do."

"I do. I do love Jesus."

"It says in the Bible, 'Ye must be born again.' Do you remember a day when you did not love Jesus?" asked Mother.

Rachel's mouth turned down at the corners. "No. Mommy. Does that mean I can't have two birthdays?"

"No. If you love Jesus it means He has adopted you. He is your adopted Father even if you can't remember the exact date you were 'born again.' Since you don't know the day, why not let you choose your own adopted birthdate?"

"Any day I want?"

"Any day."

"I want to think about it."

"When you have decided, let me know."

"What about Sunny?"

"He is too young yet to understand about Jesus. We will wait until he is a little older for him to decide."

"And Judy?"

"Judy knows the exact date she became adopted

by God. It happened on September the first. She told me about her decision that very day."

"Let's celebrate that birthdate, too."

"That means we will have to bake three birthday cakes a year for Judy," said Mommy.

"I'll help, I'll help," shouted Rachel.

Mommy smiled as she shook the flour from her cannister. "In this family it is impossible to have too many birthdays."

# Please Face Me

"For God so loved the world, that He gave His only begotten Son, that whosoever believeth in Him should not perish, but have everlasting life." John 3:16

"Mother, what is a cross?"

"It can be many things," said Mother. "It can be a mark like this." She drew two lines and made them, as she explained cross each other.

"That's a kiss," said Rachel.

"Yes, it is."

"Then there is a cross that looks like this." Mother drew another two lines, but this time the one line went straight up and down. The other one cut across it close to the top.

"That's the cross I mean," said Rachel.

"That kind of cross was used by people who lived when Jesus did. They were called Romans. They used it to punish bad people. They killed them by nailing them to these two pieces of wood made in the shape of this kind of cross. The hands were nailed one on each side. The two feet they tied together and with one big nail they fastened them here." She pointed to the base of the cross.

"Did it hurt?"

"You know how it felt when you hit your thumb

43

with a hammer."

"Oh, it ouchied."

"Just pounding the nails through the flesh of the hands and feet was agony. But after the bad man was nailed to the cross, the up-and-down plank with him nailed onto it was lifted to the sky and the foot end put into a deep hole, so that the cross would not wobble. Then the bad man had to hang there in the hot sun upon his cross until he finally died. Sometimes it took all day. They called this way of punishment crucifixion."

"Jesus died on a cross."

"Yes. He lived when the Romans were in power, and this was their form of punishment for certain bad deeds."

"Was Jesus bad?"

"No. You know He was perfect. But Jesus did become bad for us. On the cross He took upon Himself the badness of the world for whom He died. The Bible says in 2 Corinthians 5:21, "For He hath made Him to be sin for us, who knew no sin; that we might be made the righteousness of God in Him.' Do you know what God the Father did when Jesus Christ died on the cross?"

"He cried?" asked Rachel.

"That's a good guess," said Mother. "But God the Father did not cry; it was Jesus who cried out, 'My God, my God, why hast Thou forsaken Me?'

God turned His back on Jesus at that moment, for in that moment of time the heavenly Father did not see the beloved Son, but only the sickening sins of the world. God never turns His face toward sin. Jesus is the only person who has lived on this earth who during His lifetime was God-forsaken. Our problem is why? Why would God do this to His beloved one?"

"Did God love Jesus?"

"Very, very much. That is what beloved means. So we are sure that, if it had been possible, God the Father would never have been so unloving as to let His Beloved die in such a dreadful way. Let me give you a hint. This death on the cross has stumped many grown-ups, so don't feel sad that you cannot answer it right away. Does God love you?"

"Jesus loves me, this I know, for the Bible tells me so," answered Rachel.

"This is the hard part. Will He ever turn His back on you?"

"I hope not."

"You can do more than hope. You can know He won't because, if you truly believe, He has already done so to Jesus. You see, Rachel, your sins were some of the ones that Jesus took to the cross with Him. God turned His back on you and your sins when He died on the cross."

Rachel smiled and Mother knew why. They shared a secret. At night Rachel slept across the hall from Mother in her own bedroom. She was very brave when it was light, but at night she did not like the dark, and she had made Mommy promise never to go to sleep unless her face was turned toward her. Sometimes when Rachel awakened in the middle of the night and was frightened she would call out, "Are you looking at me, Mother?" And Mother would call back, "Yes, my face is turned toward you." For Mother remembered just before she fell asleep to turn on her left side so that her face would be turned toward Rachel. She tried never to fall asleep with her back turned. A promise is a promise. It was a private secret between them.

Rachel understood about God and her now. It made her happy that God would never turn His back on her. But it made her feel very sad for Jesus.

"Let's go over it all once again. This is the most important teaching in the Bible. Without it we do not have a gospel or good news to give anybody. Why won't God ever turn His back on you?"

"Because He turned His back on Jesus."

"Keep going," said Mother. "God turned His back on Jesus for . . . come on now. You almost have it. For whom did Jesus die on the cross?"

"For me."

"Yes, for you, for me, for everyone who will lay their sins on Jesus. Now He will never, ever have to turn His back on us. How about saying John 3:16 for me?"

"Help me, Mother."

"Let us say it together. 'For God so loved the world, that He gave His only begotten Son, that whosoever believeth in Him should not perish, but have everlasting life.'

"That is why," said Mother, "the Roman cross, that horrible way of punishment, has become so precious to us. Without it, God would not be able to turn His face toward us."

"The cross," said Rachel, "is like the other cross. It is a kiss from God."

# One, Two, Three, Four

"Thou shalt have no other gods before Me." Exodus 20:3

Rachel hated to see Sunny put into the playpen. He would put up a great shout and kick his fat legs which would rather be free to crawl about.

"Must we, Mother?"

"Well, not if you watch him every moment."

It all worked well for a while, but finally Rachel came in to where Mother was peeling potatoes. "I'm tired of watching, Mother." Right on her heels crawled gurgling Sunny. In one minute he reached under the table and grabbed the tail of Xanthippe who howled. The cat loved Sunny, but her tail hurt, so she spat at him while he held on. Sunny had a firm grip. Mother petted one end of Xanthippe while she forced Sunny's hand open at the other end. A very angry cat shot out of the kitchen.

"Sunny does not know any better," said Mommy, "and he just crawls smiling and cooing into danger. I don't blame you for being tired. You have been a good baby-sitter for a long time, and until I am finished in the kitchen Sunny will just have to be fenced in."

Sunny was placed into the pen with a new toy

and settled down after a few shrieks to gurgle over his rubber lion.

"Why don't you fence me in?" asked Rachel.

"You are fenced in," said Mother. You are big enough to see a make-believe fence. You know what you are not allowed to do. We Christians are all fenced in. We can't go whenever and wherever we wish."

"Are you fenced in too, Mother?"

"Yes, indeed. Do you know where I would be right this very minute if I weren't fenced in?"

"Where?"

"Anywhere but at this kitchen table peeling potatoes. I don't like peeling potatoes. But if I did only what I liked to do, you would have nothing but cakes and fudge to eat. I find it very dull to peel potatoes."

"What does the Bible say about peeling potatoes, Mother?"

"The Bible doesn't talk about potatoes, Rachel. They did not eat potatoes in Bible times. But it does say in Ecclesiastes 9:10, 'Whatsoever thy hand findeth to do, do it with thy might.' There is a chapter in the Bible, Exodus 20, that has the main fences listed. Why don't we, every time Mother peels potatoes, think about one of them? That would help Mother enjoy potato-peeling time. Do you know what the ten fence posts are, Rachel?

What do we call them?"

"The Ten Commandments."

"Good. 'Commandment' simply means what to do or not do. I command you or tell you to do or not do certain things. Here is where God the Father tells us what to do and not do. The first one is found in Exodus 20:3: 'Thou shalt have no other gods before Me.' When I was a little girl, I used to think that if I put God first I could put all the other gods in a row after Him. But this is not what 'before' means. If I say to you, 'Rachel, come out from under the table; I want you before me,' that means I want you where I can see you—it means 'in my presence.' It is not 'before Me' as if there were one, two, three, four, and God is number one. It means 'in God's sight.' While you were under the table I could not see you. Does that mean that God could not? You were not in my presence, but can you ever get out of God's presence?"

"What about Adam and Eve?"

"They tried to hide from God. Did they win?"

"They tried to play hide and seek with God," said Rachel, "but God tagged them."

"When I was a little girl we had a motto hanging by the telephone in our home. It read, 'Christ is the head of this home, the unseen guest at every meal, the silent listener to every conversation.' Can you hide from God, Rachel?"

"No."

"There is a verse in the Bible in Proverbs 15:3 which says, 'The eyes of the Lord are in every place, beholding the evil and the good.' Mother does not have eyes in the back of her head. You can hide from me, but you can never escape God's presence. You are always before Him, so that when the Bible says you are to have no other gods before Him, it means you shall have no other gods. Now what about these other gods? When Mommy was your age she lived in a land across the seas. Her parents were missionaries. And in this land of India she had a dear little friend whose name was Ganesha. She was named after an idol her parents and she worshiped. He was Ganesh, the elephant god. He had a head like an elephant. Now Ganesha had other gods before God. She worshiped the god after whom she was named and many, many more. My father would say that in India there were more gods than people. I did not put Ganesh in the presence of God. Does that mean that I kept this commandment?"

"Yes."

"It seems as if I did. But I didn't."

"You didn't?"

"All the commandments have what we call a deeper meaning. Let me give you a hint. Whom do you love best, Rachel?"

"You and Daddy and Judy and Sunny. Must I choose?"

"No. Not among us. You love all of us differently, but we hope you love one as much as the next. But this is the big question: do you love Jesus more than you love Daddy or Mommy or Judy or Sunny or yourself? You do not have to answer this very moment. But think about it. Mother loves you all so very much that sometimes she has to think very hard about this fence. Do I love my family more than I love God? If I do, I have other gods before Him. God wants me to love my family, but He does not even want someone like you, love, to be a god in His presence. Why, do you suppose, should we love God most of all?"

"Jesus saved me," said Rachel.

"That is the most important reason. Jesus died for you. Mother and Daddy would gladly die for you, little one, but we couldn't die for your sins. You could never get to heaven by our deaths. We are not good enough to die for our own sins, let alone the sins of our family. There is another reason to put God first. Even before Jesus came, at the very beginning of the Bible, what did God do for us?"

"Adam. Is it something about Adam?"

"Yes. God made Adam. If there had been no Adam there would have been no Rachel. So He is our God because He made us. Another reason why we should love God best is one you will be happy about. You know that as a family we like to be together. But we cannot always be in the same place at the same time. Sometimes you are away visiting your friends. Sometimes Mommy and Daddy go out for an evening. But who never, ever leaves us for a second?"

"Jesus."

"So we love Jesus because He saves us, He made us, and He never leaves us—He keeps us. There are many, many more reasons why we should love God best, but even if we did not know why we should, let me start our lessons on the do's and don'ts of God by saying this. God tells us not to put other gods before Him. That is enough reason to put Him first."

"Mommy," said Rachel. "Look at all the potatoes you have peeled."

"Dear me!" said Mother. "My paring knife was going as fast as my tongue. I did not notice what I was doing. We will certainly have to have company for dinner to eat them up. Why don't you telephone Suzy and ask her for dinner?"

"Will you help me to be sure I get Suzy? My fingers get stuck in the telephone holes."

"I most certainly will," said Mother, wiping her wet hands on the paper towel.

# The Christmas Tree

"Thou shalt not make unto thee any graven image."
Exodus 20:4

The family always bought a live fir tree for their
Christmas tree. This way they could plant it after
Christmas and remember Christmases past. The
yard was filling up with fir trees.

"We will be living in the Black Forest soon,"
said Mother.

"Like Gretel," said Rachel.

"My father used to say to me, 'You plant flow-
ers for yourself. You plant trees for the next
generation.' We are taking very good care of the
next generation."

Mother especially loved the Christmas tree.
When she was a little girl, she explained, she had
had to give up having a tree. One year they had
gone into the forest in the jungles of India to cut
down a tree for their living room. There were no fir
trees, but they had found a small tree with lots of
leaves. They had such fun stringing popcorn for
garlands. But the Indians did not understand what
they were doing. They had said to her father,
"What sort of holy tree do you worship?" They did
have a sacred tree, the "peepul tree." They would

54

put food out for the gods under its branches. They had thought that the Christmas tree was an idol, and that Grandmother's delicious fudge was for the gods.

Mother told Rachel about this time in her girlhood as they shelved their potato peeling for the day to make Christmas cookies.

"How sad," said Rachel.

"Yes. But in a way it was good for us children. We learned early not to do anything that would cause another child of God to stumble. It was good for our souls to have to give up the Christmas tree. It was especially necessary for us because as well as having neighbors who were Hindus who worshiped idols, we had neighbors who were Muslims. Muslims did not worship idols. They believed in the Ten Commandments also. Their prophet, Mohammed, took much of his teaching from the Old Testament, and they were especially careful to keep this commandment, the second of the ten. 'Thou shalt not make unto thee any graven image.' They would not even allow themselves to be photographed, because this would be a graven image.

"We did not photograph them. We respected their customs. But do you think this is what God meant in this commandment, Rachel?"

"I hope not," said Rachel, who had asked for a

camera for Christmas.

"The rest of the verse explains what God meant. Let me read it to you while we set the timer for the cookies. In Exodus 20:5 God explains the commandment: 'Thou shalt not bow down thyself to them, nor serve them.' We are not bowing down to our Christmas tree nor to our snapshot album, so we are allowed to have both of these and not sin. We did not wave our own photographs around to offend our neighbors, so we did not need to give up our cameras in India. But it is very hard to hide a lighted Christmas tree, so we did not practice this custom, in order not to harm what the Bible calls the weaker brother. But don't feel sorry for Mommy. We sang Christmas carols. We filled stockings at Christmas. And the most fun was that we wrapped packages for all the Christian children. In the missionary barrels people sent to us they would tuck pencils, and tablets, and dolls with the clothing. We saw to it that each little child had a dress and a toy."

"A dress, Mommy? Did the boys like that?"

"They did not care. It made no difference to them. It was something pretty to wear. Most of them were too poor to have any clothes. By the way, their mothers were very practical with these dresses. They made the children wear them inside out during the week. Then on Sunday they let them wear them right side out. We had no pretty wrapping paper as we have in America, so we used newspaper and string. But we wrapped them. Half the fun of Christmas is wrapping the gifts and unwrapping them."

"I am so glad I live in America. I would not like to have a Christmas without a Christmas tree."

"And I am glad I don't have to tell you what my Daddy told me, Rachel: 'No Christmas tree this Christmas.' How wonderful to live in a Christian land where most of the people do not fall down and worship gods of mud and stone and trees. But what are you doing, Rachel?"

"I am putting some of my Christmas money into my mission box. I feel sorry for the little children living in such a land. Maybe the money will help them. Maybe their mothers can fill their stockings with toys this money will buy."

"And maybe some of it can be used to tell the children what is most important of all, that God is not a god which you can make with your own hands. We read in Isaiah 40:19 and 20:

> As for the idol, a craftsman casts it,
> a goldsmith fashions chains of silver.
> He who is too impoverished for such an
> offering selects a tree that does not rot;

> He seeks out for himself a skillful
> craftsman to prepare an idol that will
> not totter.

People want something to worship even if they have to make a god with their own hands. Our missionaries take the gospel to them, the good news that God is a spirit and that they who worship Him must worship Him in spirit and in truth."

"Mommy, you know something? This is a commandment I can keep."

"Yes," said Mother, "outwardly. But all these commandments have an inward meaning also. If you look at them quickly it seems that many of them we can keep. But if we take a second look, we may be breaking them and not even knowing that we are. The First Commandment tells us whom we are to worship. This commandment tells us how we are to worship. God does not leave this up to ourselves. He tells us not to make idols. In America, because it is what we call 'a Christian nation,' very few people worship idols made of hands; but we do feel we have a right to decide how God should be worshiped. Suzy's mother told me the other day that once upon a time she felt she did not need to go to church. She preferred to go out into the woods and talk to God under the trees.

Now, it is wonderful to see God in the beauty of
the woodlands, but when she does not worship
God in the way He has said she should, by meeting
with other Christians in His church, she is not
obeying the commandment which tells her how to
worship. She was breaking the Second Commandment. Through Suzy, your friend and her daughter,
she is learning that she cannot make a god out of
her own imagination. She comes to church and she
has stopped breaking the Second Commandment."

"Does she still go to the woods, Mother?"

"Indeed she does. But she does not go there
when she should be in the church."

"I like Suzy's mother."

"I do too. She is a very honest woman. She
wants to do what is right. She loves God."

"She likes children and animals."

"That makes her about perfect," said Mother.

# By Hamlet

"Thou shalt not take the name of the Lord thy God in vain."
Exodus 20:7


"Potato-peeling time," called Rachel, pulling up her little rocker that Grandmother had given her. It was just right for a little girl. Her feet reached the floor. And she could even wiggle while she listened, and rock back and forth.

Daddy understood how hard it was to sit still during church. He felt sorry for her, but maybe that was because he was far away in the pulpit. It was always Mommy who had to sit in the pew and keep her from wiggling. Daddy said sitting still was hard work. He told her he had once read about "the tremendous activity of a small child sitting still." That was why Rachel loved her rocker, he would say, because she could actively sit still.

"I am ready for the do's and don'ts of God," called out Rachel, rocking back and forth.

Mother pulled out the sack of potatoes and began, "Third Commandment: 'Thou shalt not take the name of the Lord thy God in vain.' Do you know what 'in vain' is?" asked Mother, throwing a spoiled potato into the trash can. "I hope this bad potato hasn't had time to reach the rest. This is why we want you to be careful not to be yoked to bad people. It is hard not to get spoiled yourself if you are smack bang against other bad people all the time. You are to stay in the world, for the world needs your light, but that does not mean you are to jump into a bag together with bad potatoes. But I am off the subject."

"That's okay. I forgive you," said Rachel.

"What does 'in vain' mean?"

"Vain is looking in the mirror," said Rachel.

"That is what we say today when somebody is proud of his looks and keeps looking in the mirror. We say he is vain. But the language we speak changes. Grandmother uses words we don't use in her way. To be 'square,' for example, meant, in Grandma's day, to be perfect. In a square each side is exactly the same. It is perfect. Look at one of Sunny's blocks. They are perfectly square. Today, square is used to describe people who think only of themselves. As one author said of a lady in his book she was bordered on the north, south, east and west by herself. If you, Rachel, were bordered on the north, south, east, and west by Rachel, you would be called square [in 1974]. That would not be a compliment. But in Grandmother's day, if you were a good girl—kind and loving and honest—you would be square. You know the Cub Scouts promise to be square, meaning it the way Grandma means it. Judy's friend, Bobby, did not want to be a Cub Scout because he did not want to promise to be square. He was thinking of the way we use the word today.

"This is why all the Bibles in our home do not have exactly the same words. God gave the Old Testament to the Hebrew people, and each of these Hebrew words was inspired by God. But we are not all able to read the Hebrew Old Testament like Daddy, so we have to trust the students who have taken the Hebrew and written it for us word for word in our own language. These students have tried to be as true to the first Old Testament as possible. This Bible that Mommy loves so much was written in English for us in 1611; that was long before Grandmother was born. And if words have changed from her time to ours, you see how important it is that we understand the words written so many hundreds of years ago. So students keep making new translations of the older words, and try to make it easier for us."

"Do any of them use crayon words?"

"Yes, a man named Kenneth Taylor uses easy words. He gives the thought of each verse, but not always word for word."

"What does he say about 'in vain'?"

"He says, 'You shall not use the name of Jehovah your God irreverently.' When you are reverent, you are thoughtful. Using God's name in vain means using it without thinking of what you are saying."

"Jenny's Daddy does it all the time," said Rachel.

"People do," said Mother. "I have never heard Jenny take God's name in vain."

"She did once. When she fell off the swing she said, 'My God.' Her Mother picked her up and said, 'I heard you say *My God*. Jenny Harper, were you praying?' Jenny said she wasn't."

"What did her Mother say?"

"She said, 'We use God's name only when we are praying.' "

"That was a good way to explain it to Jenny. Does Jenny still take God's name in vain?"

"No, but Mr. Harper does all the time. Mommy, why doesn't Mrs. Harper tell Mr. Harper about it?"

"Maybe she does in private," said Mother. "You are old enough to understand that Mr. Harper does many things that we hope Jenny and you won't do. You see, God does not force anyone to keep His commandments. The fence is there. You see how Sunny already is trying to climb out of his playpen. Many people climb over the fences of God."

"Has Mr. Harper climbed over the fence?"

"If what you say is true, he has—if he does not keep this commandment. But what is more important to us is: do *we* keep this commandment? Is this one that we don't have to worry about? Remember, I caught you the last time!"

"Is the answer that yes, I jump over this fence, too?" asked Rachel.

"Yes, it is. Do you know why? I do not believe you will take God's name in vain the way Jenny did very easily because we reverence His name in this house and you don't hear God's name sprinkled like salt and pepper in our talk. But there are other ways to take God's name in vain. Let me explain.

"When I was a little girl in India this was an easy commandment for me to understand, because no woman in India would even take her husband's name in vain. It would be considered rude to do so. When I asked Manmutti, my 'ayah' or baby-sitter, what her husband's name was she would not tell me. She would describe him as the father of her sons, but she would never say his real name. His name was 'Faith' in her language. When she recited Bible verses it sounded funny because she would always leave the word 'faith' out of the Scripture. We all understood it was out of respect for her husband. She would not take his name in vain.

"Later on in this country I had a friend whose father was a Jewish rabbi. He would not even write out the name for God, 'Jehovah.' He would use a sign or symbol instead. When he saw this sign for

Jehovah he would not even then read it, but he would put in an entirely different word, 'Elohim,' which means 'the Lord.' God's name was too holy to spell or pronounce."

"Then you don't break this commandment, Mother."

"I am afraid that I do, dear. Although I do not use God's name the way Mr. Harper does—we call that 'swearing'—I do take God's name in vain because I use it thoughtlessly. Sometimes in church when I say the Lord's Prayer, I have said it so often before that, instead of praying, I wake up for the 'amen' and know that I have not been paying attention to what I have been saying. I have been taking the Lord's name in vain."

"I do that sometimes with the 'Now I lay me's,' " said Rachel.

"I know you do, because some nights you ask to say them over again."

"Like Christopher Robin," said Rachel.

"Exactly," said Mother, singing one of Rachel's favorite songs from Winnie the Pooh. " 'Little boy kneels at the foot of the bed.' You remember all the things that take Christopher Robin's mind away from his prayers, even his nanny's dressing gown."

"He must have had his eyes open."

"Yes. It helps us not to take God's name in vain if we close our eyes when we pray and shut out interesting things we can see. Dear little Christopher Robin was breaking the Third Commandment."

"My! Commandments are hard to keep," said Rachel. "Even Christopher Robin jumped this fence, and he was such a good boy. He loved animals."

Loving animals was what made a good person perfect in Rachel's eyes. "Speaking of animals, see how proud Hamlet is of his name," said Mother. "He knows it. A name is a very special thing. We should never use even a dog's name carelessly. If I kept saying, 'By Hamlet,' all the time, Hamlet would prick up his ears and come running because he would think I was calling him. How angry God must get when we keep yelling His name and we don't mean it."

"Why are you cutting the potatoes in thin pieces, Mommy?"

"I thought we would have potatoes au gratin tonight. You go to the refrigerator and get the au gratin for me. Can you guess what au gratin is? It is on the first shelf. It is a French word for . . ."

"Cheese," said Rachel.

"I will let you use the shredder carefully and you can sprinkle the potatoes with cheese."

"I love potatoes 'o gotten,' " said Rachel.

"I do too," said Mother.

# Wholly Wholly Holy

"Remember the Sabbath day, to keep it holy."
Exodus 20:8

Rachel sat up in her bed and sniffed. Goody! Mommy was baking cinnamon rolls for breakfast. Rachel looked forward to Sunday breakfast. Mother always said Sunday was the best day of the week. And the family started the happy day with a good meal.

Rachel put on her slippers and bathrobe and sang "The Yellow Rose of Texas" as she ran down the stairs. She was still singing as she opened the door into the kitchen. Mother smiled at her and stooped down to get her good-morning kiss. "What were you singing, dear?"

Rachel placed her hand over her mouth. "Oh, I forgot! That wasn't exactly a Jesus song, and today is Jesus' day."

"I like to hear you sing," Mother said. "Why not sing that pretty song you learned last Sunday in Sunday school?"

Rachel was singing, "Can a little child like me praise the Father fittingly," when the rest of the family came down to breakfast.

Daddy came in first. When he stooped to kiss

her, she stroked his cheek. It was smooth. "I shaved my fur, kitten," Daddy teased. It was a family joke. When people said to Rachel, "You look just like your Daddy," she had always answered, "But I don't have fur on my face." She had always called Daddy's beard "fur."

Jonathan was gurgling in his crib in the bedroom. Daddy went in and carried him back in his bassinet.

Last of all came Judy. Why is it, thought Rachel, that the older you get the longer you want to sleep? She couldn't bear to stay in bed a moment after her eyes opened.

Daddy pushed in Mommy's chair. Then they all sat down, folded their hands, and sang the grace they saved for Sunday mornings together:

*Be present at our table, Lord.*
*Be here and everywhere adored.*
*These mercies bless, and grant that we*
*May feast in Paradise with Thee.*

"Daddy," said Judy, "Teacher said that we should try to watch a program this evening on TV that she thought we would all enjoy. It is *Treasure Island.*"

"It is a good story, Judy. It is still one of my favorites. It is too bad it has to be shown on

Sunday evening. But you know that today is the Lord's day. And on this one day of the week we listen only to religious programs. Now if it were *The Lion, the Witch and the Wardrobe*, we would all tune in."

"Why," asked Rachel, "do they have all the children's programs on Sunday?"

"You forget, Rachel, the many pleasant programs you listen to on weekdays," said Daddy. But it is true that often very good children's plays and books are produced on Sunday evening. The reason for this is that children do not have school on Sunday, and they have time to sit and listen to them. It is sad that because of this we feel the Sabbath-day commandment is broken. And even sadder is the fact that people, many of them, don't seem to know even that this is one of the Ten Commandments."

"But teacher said . . ." Judy turned to her father.

"Teacher doesn't go to our church," said Rachel.

Daddy laughed.

"None of my friends keep the Sabbath," said Judy.

"What other people do, or don't do, is never any reason for us to do or not do something. They must do what they think is right. For us our guide is not how many people keep the Sabbath day holy but what we understand the Bible to teach when it says, 'Remember the Sabbath day, to keep it holy.' "

"What the Bible teaches," echoed Judy.

"Remember that, and you will never go wrong. Never think in unison, or with the crowd, even the crayon crowd."

"Doesn't Judy's teacher believe in the Bible, Daddy?"

"Yes, she does. I am very glad you asked that question, Rachel. It will help us understand a very important truth. The Bible is the Word of God. God makes no mistakes. But we who read the Bible can. When Judy's teacher reads that commandment she thinks keeping the Sabbath holy means resting and relaxing from duties she does on other days of the week, as well as worshipping God. I think keeping the Sabbath holy means keeping it wholly holy. You pronounce 'wholly' the same way as 'holy,' but it means something very special. It means 'completely,' or, to use a crayon crowd word, it means 'only.' I think the Sabbath is God's holy day and we keep it holy wholly, or only, for Him, except for necessary duties. Now let me ask you a question: can Judy's teacher and Daddy both be right?"

"No," said Rachel.

"That is my little logician," said Daddy. "Well,

then, which one is right?"

"You, Daddy."

Daddy laughed. "That is not logic, sweetheart, that is love! But, Rachel, even if you thought Judy's teacher was right, so long as you were our little girl living with us you would keep our rules. So here we have it. Either Judy's teacher is right and I am wrong, or . . ."

"You are right, and she is wrong," finished Daddy's little logician.

"We are both sinners. We both make mistakes. And we must both live by our understanding of the Book. Remember the problem lies with us. The mistakes are ours. The Bible is never wrong.

"People have," said Daddy, "many different ideas of what it means to keep the Sabbath day holy. The other day I visited a dear little lady in the home for the aged. It was Sunday and she was tuned in to a television station watching the Pittsburgh Pirates play baseball. She very graciously turned off the set when I came in, but she was not at all embarrassed to have me catch her with it turned on. But while we were talking together she showed me a beautiful afghan she was crocheting for her granddaughter. It was almost finished.

" 'Will you finish it today?' I asked.

"She was shocked. 'Pastor, you know I don't work on the Sabbath day.'

"She felt that keeping the Sabbath day holy meant only doing no work on that day. And before both you girls decide to change sides and join this grandma, let me ask you another question, Why do we have so many different denominations in our small town? Do we not believe in the same God, the same Savior, and the same Bible?"

"Yes," said Judy. "But we read the Bible our own way."

"I hope not," said Daddy, "but we do try to read the Bible very carefully, with our own minds. We do not, I am sorry to say, come out with the same answers. And so long as we don't, we must of course follow what we feel is the Bible way.

"Here is a story for you, Judy. A little girl came home from Sunday school and told her Daddy that her teacher had said that Jesus was a Jew.

" 'He was,' said her Daddy.

" 'How can he be,' said the little girl, 'when God was a Presbyterian?' "

"*Is* God a Presbyterian, Daddy?" asked Rachel.

"If I thought He were a Methodist, I would be a Methodist. Does that answer your question?"

"And Presbyterians feel we must keep the Sabbath day," sighed Judy.

"At least this Presbyterian does," said Daddy. "Now what do you suppose I have in that shopping bag by my briefcase?"

"A surprise, a surprise! Is it for me?" asked Rachel.

"How did you guess?" teased Daddy. "Yes, one for you and one for Judy."

Rachel brought the shopping bag over to her father. He reached in and gave each child a package.

Judy opened hers first. It was a book, *Through Gates of Splendor*, by Elisabeth Elliot. "Daddy, thank you so very much. Mother was reading me about the martyrdom of Mr. Elliot. I am so thrilled to get the whole story."

Rachel was having trouble with the Scotch tape on her bundle. Finally she tore it open. Inside was a beautiful book of Bible pictures. "I can't wait to read mine! Isn't it too bad Sunny is too little to read? But I will show him my pictures."

Rachel had learned the letters in the alphabet and could guess some words. She loved to "read."

"I thought perhaps you would enjoy these today," said Daddy.

"Another cinnamon roll, anyone?" asked Mother.

"Please," said Rachel and Judy together, laughing.

There are many things we cannot do, thought Rachel. But there are many wonderful things we can do. The most important thing is to do what will please God. This is what Rachel was thinking. But she was too little to say it. Instead she just took a big bite out of her roll and smiled a sweet smile at her family.

# Mother Knows Best

"Honor thy father and thy mother." Exodus 20:12


"Let's not peel potatoes today, Mommy. Let's have baked potatoes and I can scrub them."

"That would be wonderful," said Mother. "You do the work and I shall sit in your rocker and watch you."

"Will you fit in my rocking chair?" Rachel looked worried.

"I can get in. You may have to pull me out. My! This feels so good," said Mother as she rocked back and forth. Rachel climbed up on her little stool that helped her be Mommy-size at the sink. She took the vegetable brush from the drain and started to scrub the potatoes.

"Our commandment today is the fifth, 'Honor thy father and thy mother.'"

"What does 'honor' mean?" asked Rachel.

"It is always a good idea to let the Bible explain itself," said Mother. "In Ephesians 6:1–2 we read, 'Children, obey your parents in the Lord for this is right. Honor thy father and mother; which is the first commandment with promise.' You know what 'obey' is."

"Yes. If I don't obey I get spanked."

"Let me tell you a strange story about a lady who did not obey. In this case it was her husband, and she did the right thing. It was a beautiful queen whose name was Vashti. Her husband was a great king and he was giving a banquet in honor of his important guests. He drank too much wine and got drunk. When a man is drunk he does many silly things. Sometimes when he has recovered from being drunk he does not even remember what he has done. I remember one time riding on a street-car and seeing a man who had drunk too much; he was acting like a fool and we were all laughing at him. He was very well dressed. He looked as if he were a banker. He reminded me of Mr. Cooper in our church who is an elder and very dignified. This man thought he was being very clever. I remember wishing I had a movie camera and the man's address. I would have taken movies of him and sent them to him. If he had ever seen how stupid he looked, I don't believe he would ever have become drunk again."

"I drink a lot, and I don't get drunk, Mommy."

Mother sighed. "Dear me! That just goes to show even mommies don't explain enough. I sometimes wonder how you children ever learn anything from us. We just rattle on and expect you to keep up. Let me try to explain, honey. There are some drinks which are good for you, like milk, for example. You can drink lots and lots of milk. You can get stuffed, but you won't get drunk on milk. Other drinks are made in a special way; grown-ups call it "made by fermentation." If you drink too much of these you get drunk. Not only will you act silly on the outside, but your brains, the part of your body you use in thinking, will be harmed on the inside.

"When I was a little girl in a boarding school in India they had an awful way of curing us when we got a tummy ache. They would bring big jugs of water, and we would have to drink and drink and drink until our tummies turned somersaults and everything would come up. The idea behind this was that something in our stomachs was making us sick, and that if we got it up and out we would be well again.

"I can tell you, sweetheart, you can drink buckets and buckets of water and you will never get drunk. These drinks which make you drunk you will see in the windows of the liquor stores we pass on the way to church. They are whiskey or different types of wines, and all are drinks made of alcohol.

"Some people can drink a glass or two of these beverages and then stop before they get drunk. But other people start and can't stop. The reason we don't have any of these types of drinks around the house is that doctors say that one out of ten people just *have* to keep on drinking once they start. You never know who that tenth person will be. I may not be that one, but I would be guilty if I served someone who would be that one in ten persons who became a drunkard. But to get back to our story . . . we do go way off, don't we?"

"Isn't it fun?" said Rachel. "It's such fun to get off the subject."

"Daddy doesn't think so," said Mommy. "But we women enjoy it. To continue, this king whose name was Ahasuerus . . ."

"His name sounds like a sneeze," said Rachel.

"It does sound a little like 'Ah-choo.' At least they both start with an 'A.' Well, anyway, this drunken king thought he had a very good idea. Being drunk he could not tell the difference. It was a stupid idea. But he asked his queen to come and dance before his drunken guests, who were all as silly and drunk as he was. This would have been a disgraceful thing to do, so Vashti said, 'No.' Now, little scrubber of potatoes, was that a good 'no' or a bad 'no'?"

"Good."

"Correct. Now," said Mother, "I am not likely to get drunk and ask you to do something as stupid as that. But it is possible that I could ask you to do something that God would not like you to do. If this happens, which one of us should you obey, God or me?"

"God."

"In India, sometimes children want to become Christians and their parents say 'no.' Should they obey their parents and say 'no' to God?"

"No."

"We call that a 'Vashti' no. or a 'good' no. That is why I like this verse in Ephesians which explains the commandment. It says we are to obey, but only in the Lord. In other words, if what Mommy and Daddy ask you to do does not go against any of God's commandments, then you must obey them. And parents are only the first step in the ladder of obedience. In the Bible we are taught as Christians to obey those who have the rule over us. With Vashti it was Ahasuerus . . ."

"Bless you," said Rachel.

Mother laughed. "In school it is the teachers. With Daddy, as a preacher, it is the session of the church. But remember, it is always in the Lord. This verse also says this is the first commandment with promise. You see, in Exodus this commandment is followed by the words, 'that thy days may be long upon the land which the Lord thy God giveth thee.' You actually may live longer if you are obedient to your parents. I was thinking as I read this verse just now of poor Joel Winthrop in the hospital. You know what happened to him, don't you?"

"He rode his bike on the highway."

"His Daddy had told him over and over again to stay off that road. He did not obey and now he is very seriously hurt and in the hospital. He was hit by a car. There is an old saying that has been handed down from mother to mother to mother. It is 'Mother knows best.' This goes for daddies too. It is just that mothers are more often with you children because daddies have to be out earning the bread and butter to put on the table. Mothers are more often around to be obeyed. Mother, we know, can be wrong. But most of the time she does know best. For one thing she has lived longer and she has had more time to learn to know best. When she says, 'Don't do something,' don't. But even when you are smarter than Mother is, as a Christian child, you are to obey. The only time you can say a 'Vashti' no is when she tells you to do something against the Lord's teachings.

"You have those potatoes sparkling," Mother interrupted herself. "Let's put them in the oven. Me oh my! You are going to have to pull me out of this beautiful rocker. Like Winnie the Pooh, bear with little brain, I am stuck."

Rachel dried her hands on a paper towel and came running. With much puffing and pulling,

Mommy finally bounced out of the rocker like a cork out of a bottle.

"Remind me never to sit there again," said Mother. "But it was fun while it lasted. This has been such a restful potato-peeling time. Thank you for the use of your rocking chair."

"You're welcome," said Rachel.

# The Sleepy Blanket

"Thou shalt not kill." Exodus 20:13

"Mommy," asked Rachel, "why does baby put the silky edge of his blanket in his mouth before he goes to sleep?"

"It comforts him," said Mother. "He is becoming as attached to his 'sleepy blanket' as you once were. Do you know that when you were little we always had to be sure, before we took a trip, that we packed your special pink blanket? Even when you slept in motels you had to have this blanket closest to you. You know your favorite cartoon book about Peanuts has baby brother Linus always walking around holding onto his baby blanket. I remember seeing one cartoon where Linus's mother had done the laundry and had washed his 'sleepy blanket' along with the other blankets and sheets. She had hung it together with the others out on the clothesline. The cartoonist had drawn Linus out in the yard holding onto his blanket until it dried.

"I read the other day about a monkey in a zoo who would not let the zoo keeper take away his blanket. The baby monkey kept dragging the blanket around in the mud and it was getting dirtier and dirtier. The zookeeper was afraid it might catch on a limb of a tree while the monkey was jumping and the baby would get hurt. He tried to get it away from him, but the baby would not let go. He just played tug-of-war with the zookeeper. Finally the man thought of a clever way out of his problem. He took a pair of scissors and each day he cut away a piece of the blanket. Snip, snip, he went, a little at a time, until all that was left of the blanket was a tiny square piece that the monkey held in his little fist. This the zookeeper let him keep and they both were happy.

"To Sunny and to the monkey, that blanket is a sign of love. They must both remember some time in their past when they were cuddled in a warm blanket. Everybody needs to be loved. Everybody needs to remember the times when they were cuddled. This is good. What should it teach us, Rachel, about love? How should we be toward one another? How should you feel toward Daddy and Mommy and Judy and Sunny and Suzy and all the others in your world?"

"I should love you."

"Yes. Love and love and love. The Bible tells us we should love our neighbors as ourselves. 'Our neighbor' means simply other people. My, how much we love 'me'! If we loved others that much wouldn't this be a beautiful world?"

"Mommy, you are peeling potatoes today, and we are not talking about the Ten Commandments."

"Maybe we are, and you don't know it. You remember we call the commandments the do's and don'ts of God. Each commandment we can put in the opposite way."

"Let's play that game, Mommy."

"You always like to give opposites, Rachel. Grown-ups say about the commandments that they have positive and negative sides. Positive means 'do,' and negative means 'don't do.'

"Now let us see if love can be a positive side of one of the commandments. We shall be detectives and try to find which one. But first let us see if we can tell how some of the commandments are written. I will give the commandment and you will tell me if it is positive or negative. 'Obey your father and other.' "

"Positive."

"If it were written negatively, it would say, 'Don't disobey your parents.' You know most people think the commandments are all written as don'ts, but this is not. It is a do. 'Do obey.' Now what kind of commandment is 'Don't swear'?"

"Give me a hint, Mommy."

"If it has a don't in it, it is negative."

"Negative."

"How would you make it positive?"

"Do swear."

"But that would change the idea, so it couldn't be that. We will have to try again. If we are not to take God's name in vain, it means we should use it carefully. We could write it, 'Do respect God's name.' In other words it is: 'Don't swear,' negative; 'do respect God's name,' positive.

"Now what about 'Thou shalt not kill'? Mommy sometimes says 'thee' and 'thou' because she learned the commandments that way. Let me put it in crayon words. 'Don't kill.' "

"Negative. That has a don't in it."

"Good. Now make it positive. And it won't be 'do kill.' That's a hint."

"Help me, Mommy."

"Let us take a deep look at this commandment. Jesus said it meant more than 'don't kill.' He said that if we become angry for no reason, or hated our brother, we had broken this commandment. Now let's put the commandment this way: 'Don't hate.' "

"Negative."

"Right. Now what is the opposite of hate? What are we to do?"

"Love. Do love. Positive," said Rachel.

"Yes, we are to love and love and love," said Mother.

"And love," added Rachel.

"Love without end," said Mother. "So we have been talking about a commandment today after all, the Sixth Commandment. 'Thou shalt not kill' means also that we should love one another."

"I love you, Mother."

"I love you too, Rachel. And we can't say it often enough to one another, can we?"

"Mommy, our gurgler baby is crying."

"Go look, lamb, maybe he has lost his 'sleepy blanket' again. He is lonesome for love."

"He had it, Mommy. He just wanted me, too. Nobody can have too much love," said Rachel.

# Someday My Prince Will Come

"Thou shalt not commit adultery." Exodus 20:14

"I have good news for you today, Rachel," said Mother. "You keep asking when we study the commandments, 'Is this a commandment I can keep?' And you know we have always found out that it is not. But today we have a commandment that you cannot break—not yet. It is a commandment for grown-ups. It is the Seventh Commandment: 'Thou shalt not commit adultery.'"

"Is 'dultery a common sin of grown-ups?" asked Rachel.

"You could say so. In fact, it has been said that many grown-ups think this is the only 'don't' of God. They forget there are nine other equally important commandments. The reason you can't break the commandment is that adultery is a sin only grown-ups can commit. Adultery means being unfaithful to your husband or to your wife. When you marry you promise to love only the man you marry, to live only with him. When you break this commandment, you commit adultery."

"Suzy's daddy and mother did 'dultery,

Mother."

"Suzy's mother did not. She kept her promise to be faithful to her husband. But Suzy's daddy left home to go live with another woman. I am sorry to have to say that Suzy's daddy committed adultery. Many people who stay married and don't desert their homes still break this commandment. There is a deep meaning in this commandment too, as there is in the others. Jesus tells us we can commit adultery in the heart. You can break this commandment even if only God and you know about it. That is why I want you to know about this commandment when you are little, so that when you do get married you will be true to the man you marry in your heart as well as in your life. Too many girls pick a husband using less brains that they use when they pick a brand of cereal. If they are Christian young women, their faith is not going to excuse them later if they have picked the wrong man. They will have to stay married so long as their husband is faithful to them. That means they may have to stay married to a man who doesn't want to work, or who may even be a drunkard or unkind, or just plain dull. Christians honor the promise they made before God and stay married, and they must even make their hearts be true.

"David, who slew the giant, went down under this Seventh Commandment. He took another man's wife and he broke this commandment. Then he tried to cover his sin by breaking another. He had her husband, a soldier, placed in the front of the battle where the enemy would kill him. What commandment did he break when he did this?"

Rachel counted on her fingers.

"It was the one we had just before this one. If this is the seventh, what number comes before seven?"

"Seven, six!" said Rachel, counting backwards. She had just learned to do this.

"So David started by breaking the seventh, then he went ahead and broke the sixth. That often happens when we start to break the law. It is like the dominoes you stack in a row. If you push one over it knocks down the next one in line. I wouldn't be surprised that you shall find that David broke even more than two."

"Let's see, Mommy."

"It will be a good review for us. Number one, 'No other gods.' Did he break this commandment? The woman whom David took was called Bathsheba. Do you think David put Bathsheba in God's presence?"

"Yes."

"Yes, David made her a god. So he broke number one. Number two, 'No graven images.' "

"Did he break them all?" asked Rachel.

"No," said Mommy. "I will help you that far. Did he make an image of Bathsheba?"

"No," said Rachel.

"So David did not break this one. How about the third, 'Do not swear'?"

"No. This domino did not fall," said Rachel.

"Now for the fourth. What is the fourth?"

"Tell me, Mommy."

"Keep the Sabbath day holy."

"No."

"What about the fifth? 'Honor thy father and thy mother.' "

"Yes. His mommy probably told him, as you are telling me, not to break the Seventh Commandment, and he forgot."

"You are probably right, for David came from a godly family."

"How far are we, Mommy?"

"Sixth, 'Do not kill.' "

"Yes, he broke this one. You already told me that, Mommy."

"Seventh, 'Do not commit adultery.' "

"That's the very one he started with. Yes, he broke it."

"Now we will have a preview," said Mommy. You know what a review is. That is what we have been having."

"Looking back," said Rachel.

"Try to guess what a preview is. It is looking another way."

"Sideways."

"No, guess again."

"Up."

"No."

"Down."

"No. I think there is only one other way to go. You have said backwards, sideways, up and down."

"Forward!" shouted Rachel.

"That is what a preview is. You look forward. I want you to help me with the preview. Hold up both hands and let me see all your ten fingers. No, 'don't commit adultery' is the Seventh Commandment. Put down seven fingers. How many do you have left sticking up?"

Rachel bit her tongue and counted. "One, two, three. Three."

"Now for the preview of the last three commandments. The Eighth Commandment is 'Thou shalt not steal.' The ninth is 'Thou shalt not lie.' The tenth is 'Thou shalt not want something that isn't yours.' Did David break any of these commandments?"

"Steal, yes," said Rachel. "He stole Bath—"

"Bathsheba," helped Mommy. "Now what about lying? Shall I help you? You may not know the story well enough; but he certainly acted a lie when he pretended to be a friend of Bathsheba's husband. And what about the last commandment? Someone has said it is the root of all the others, wanting something that does not rightfully belong to you. It certainly was the root trouble here. The root, honey, is the part of a plant that is underground; it is not seen, but without it there would be nothing above the ground. David wanted something that did not belong to him, and that really started the dominoes falling. So he broke commandments one, five, six, seven, eight, nine and ten. How many does that make?"

"Seven."

"He broke seven commandments while he was breaking the seventh," said Mommy.

"I always liked David," said Rachel.

"God not only liked him," said Mother, "He loved him. He called him a man after His own heart."

"How could He, Mommy?"

"I think it was because David loved Him so much. And he was sorry for his sins. This is a comfort to us. How many times we sin! But no sin, no matter how bad it is, cannot be forgiven. The important part is to ask for forgiveness and mean it. Jesus once forgave a woman who had committed adultery, saying, 'Go and sin no more.' Daddy once preached about David. He said about David that he had 'committed adultery,' but he was not an 'adulterer.' That means he did sin, but he did not keep on sinning. God forgave David these seven 'setting sins.' He would not have forgiven David if they had been 'besetting sins' about which he was doing nothing."

"Someday I am going to marry a prince," said Rachel.

"I am sure you will. If you choose wisely he will be a prince."

Rachel started to sing her favorite Cinderella song, "Someday My Prince Will Come." She had a voice, Daddy would say, like a baby lark.

"Remember, Cinderella, when you meet your prince, to keep the Seventh Commandment. Meanwhile, this is one commandment you can store away until you need it. You will be kept busy working on the other nine."

# Love Spanks

"Thou shalt not steal." Exodus 20:15

"Joel Pepper, you stop that!"

"What is Joel doing now?" asked Mother. By this time all the family knew that Joel Pepper was a little friend whom only Rachel saw. Although he had stepped out of the pages of the book, *Five Little Peppers*, that big sister Judy had read to Rachel, he had become a different little boy in Rachel's home. He was always being bad.

"Joel is taking off the lid of the cookie jar, and helping himself to a cookie."

Mother came into the kitchen and found Rachel on the kitchen stool with her fist in the cookie jar.

"Come here," said Mother. I am going to have to spank you for that. You know you do not help yourself to cookies. You must always ask first."

"But Mother, I didn't do it. Joel did."

"It was your hand in the jar."

"I was pulling Joel's out."

Mother pried open Rachel's hand. Clutched tight in it was a cookie.

"I see," said Mother. "Then this must be Joel's hand. It has a cookie in it." And Mother slapped it hard.

Rachel started to cry.

"You know, doll, when you were just a toddler, and we first started to spank you, we used to ask you—when you were bad—which hand did it. You would think, and then stretch out one hand to us, and put the other hand behind your back. We would spank the bad hand and kiss the good hand. You always acted as if the bad hand did not belong to you. Now you are blaming your play friend Joel for your badness. But you know, don't you, that Joel is really you—just as you know now that the bad hand that was spanked and the good hand that was kissed both belonged to you.

"The Bible tells us that there is within each of us an old bad man and a new good man. They are fighting each other. The Bible tells us we are to put off the old man. In other words, next time, you take care of Joel. You are responsible. You keep him out of the cookie jar. You see, Joel is your old man. If you want to call him Joel, that is all right; but just see to it that you make him behave. Otherwise you have to have outside help."

"What kind of help?"

Mother picked up a ruler. "I think this will help. You know I heard of one family that used a strap, and hung it in the living room under a motto. The motto read, 'I Need Thee Every Hour.' "

Judy laughed.

"I don't think that's funny," said Rachel. "When Mother spanks me, Sunny comforts me."

"Sunny is too little to know better," said Mother. "I know you always run to him, and he snoozles you and tries to wipe away the tears. But sister is old enough to know better. When you are naughty she knows it would be wrong to feel sorry for you when you are punished. She should feel sorry that you have been bad. But she should feel happy that you are punished."

"Why?"

"Rachel, if you were never punished, you would grow worse and worse. When you started school, perhaps your teacher would have to spank you. I would much rather you were trained in the home. That is the way God wants it to be. There is a verse in the Bible in Proverbs 13:24, 'He that spareth the rod hateth his son.' "

"What does 'spare' mean?"

"That means, in this case, 'doesn't use.' In other words, a mother or daddy that doesn't spank when a child is bad hates that child. Because if he or she loves the child he will punish, so that in the end the child will be good. If he lets his own child get away with sin, in the last days, when it is too late, he may discover that he has let his most precious treasure slip down into the very jaws of hell.

"Sometime you know how Mommy cuddles you

close and gives you little taps. We call them 'love spanks.' In a true way, every spank is a love spank."

"I still don't like them," said Rachel.

"And I still don't like to give them," said Mother. "So let's make them as few as we can."

"I heard a minister once," said Judy, "talk about two dogs in each of us, a good dog and a bad dog that were always fighting. And do you know which one wins?"

"No," said Rachel. "Which one?"

"The one we say, 'Sic 'em' to."

Everybody laughed. "But remember," Mother said, "we are grown up now and must not push the blame on a bad dog, or a bad hand, or Joel Pepper. There is only one of us, and we must always fight to grow in grace, and let us all make our own Joel Pepper be good."

"How can we, Mother? I can't do a thing with Joel. He is especially bad on the day you bake cookies. Mother, Joel says you are the best cookie-baker in the world."

"You thank Joel Pepper for me for the compliment. You tell him too that he is to ask before he helps himself to the cookies. When he takes them without asking he is breaking a commandment. Do you know which one?"

"Joel knows. It is the eighth, 'Thou shalt not steal.' He says those cookies smell so delicious. He would even like at this moment to steal another one, and he is not unspanked yet."

"If Rachel asks politely, she may have one. And then I want her to memorize a verse from the Bible that will help her. It is found in Philippians 4:13: 'I can do all things through Christ which strengtheneth me.' So she can, with Christ helping her, keep the Eighth Commandment. She has no excuse."

"I hope you heard that, Joel," said Rachel.

"I hope you heard that, Rachel," said Mother.

# Setting Sins

"Thou shalt not bear false witness." Exodus 20:16

"Mommy, let's talk about my setting sin."

Mother smiled. "I only wish it were a setting sin, Rachel. The word is 'besetting.' That means the one that is fighting you the most. If you fight back, it becomes a setting sin. Like the sun, it will set, or go down."

"Slowly," said Rachel.

"Yes," nodded Mother.

"Sometimes it sets very slowly."

"Does it help to talk about your besetting sin, darling?"

"Yes."

Mother always noticed this about Rachel. She seemed to be attached to her vices. It was very hard to let go of them. Rachel understood the word "attached." Having a professor-minister for a daddy made her speak more like a grown-up than most of her little friends. One day when her dress got caught in the car door she yelled to her mother, "Help! Help me! I'm attached to the door."

"Let's pretend," said Mother, "I don't know about your besetting sin and we will start from the beginning. You tell me about it as if I were somebody you do not know. It may help us to try this little game of make-believe. I shall be Mrs. Smith."

"Oh, Mother! Pick a fancy name."

"You pick one for me."

It was never hard for Rachel to pick a name. "You be Mrs. Narnia."

Mother pretended it was a new name that she had never known before, although she did know that was the name for the land in Rachel's favorite fairy tale book, *The Lion, the Witch and the Wardrobe* by C. S. Lewis.

"What will you be?"

"I will be Dorothy."

More often than any other storybook character, Rachel liked to be Dorothy, of *The Wizard of Oz*.

"Good morning, Dorothy," said Mother.

"Good morning, Mrs. Narnia," said Rachel.

"May I help you?" said Mrs. Narnia.

"Please. You see, I have a setting—I mean a be-setting sin."

"Sit down; we will talk about it."

"Could I have a cup of tea while we talk?" asked Dorothy.

"I am all out of tea, but would you like some orange juice?"

"That will do nicely," said Mother's visitor.

Mother came back with orange juice and cookies. It is hard to talk while eating. Rachel had been told not to talk with her mouth full. But she started once the cookie was gone and she could sip her orange juice like a lady. She wiped her mouth daintily with the flowered paper napkin Mother had given her.

"My besetting sin, Mrs. Narnia, is lying."

"Lying," echoed Mrs. Narnia. "Why do you lie so much, Dorothy?"

"You aren't supposed to know I lie so much yet, Mrs. Narnia."

"I'm sorry," said Mother.

"I lie because I enjoy it. You see, Mrs. Narnia, lies are so much more fun than the truth."

"I am listening," said Mother.

"The other day," said Dorothy, "my mother asked me where I had been. I had been hiding in a tree, but I said, 'A bad man kidnapped me.' "

"What did your mother say?" asked Mrs. Narnia.

"She asked me why he bothered to bring me back."

"What did you say?"

"I said God did. I prayed and God delivered me."

"What did your mother say?"

"She said that was an exciting story with a happy ending. But she asked where I had really been."

"And what did you say?"

"I said I was up in the apple tree."

"Now," said Mrs. Narnia, "let us think about that story. Was it a lie or was it just make-believe?"

"I wanted Mother to believe it," said Dorothy.

"If you wanted to fool your mother, Dorothy, that would be a lie. But if your mother and you both knew you were making up an exciting story, it would not be a lie."

"So a lie depends upon whom you tell it to," said Judy, who had been listening in.

"No. If you say something that is untrue, and try to make people believe it, that is a lie. Mothers are more likely to be able to tell the difference between a lie and make-believe, but you must not tell even them a story that is untrue to try to deceive them. Dorothy's trouble is that it is hard for her to tell the difference. You see, if Judy wanted to fool her mother, even though she didn't, it would be a lie. But if she told the story in fun, as make-believe between two people who are both in on the game just to make life more exciting for Mother, that would be no lie. Someday, I believe, Dorothy is going to be a storyteller and sell her stories for other people to enjoy. We want her to develop her imagination, grown-ups would say. We want her to have fun with make-believe stories, but she must work at being sure she knows the difference and that other people do too."

"I know what you mean," said Judy. "The other day Mrs. Jones told me that Rachel had told her she had been born in an igloo in Alaska."

"Did Mrs. Jones believe that story?"

"Yes," said Judy.

"I wonder what we can do about it," sighed Mother.

"Could I have another cookie?" asked Rachel.

"I wonder what we can do about it," repeated Mother.

Rachel heaved a big sigh. "I will tell Mrs. Jones I was born in Kansas."

"Where?" asked Mother.

Rachel sighed again. "I will tell Mrs. Jones I was born right here in Pennsylvania."

"That would be a good way," said Mrs. Narnia, "to turn a besetting sin into a setting sin."

"And now may I have another cookie?" said Dorothy.

"You may have two of them," said Mother. "Fighting these besetting sins works up an appetite."

# Sunny, Let Go!

"Thou shalt not covet." Exodus 20:17

Mother looked up from her typewriter to see Rachel standing near the baby's playpen. She had her small chair in one hand, pointing the four legs at the baby. Safe within his bars, baby Jonathan arched his back and gurgled.

"Rachel, what are you doing?"

"I'm taming Sunny."

Mother laughed. The big fat baby wiggling his back in the air did look like a baby lion cub. But she warned Rachel to be careful and not to get close with the chair.

"Be very careful of your baby brother, Rachel. Remember, he is very small. And God has made all of us bigger people to be caretakers of the little people. Now that big sister is away at school all day, I am counting on you to help keep baby safe."

"Is he *delicat*?"

"Well, not exactly. What made you ask?"

"You told me when you brought baby home from the hospital that we would have to be very careful of him, for he would be *delicat*."

"He was at first. You remember he could not even hold up his head. Now look at him. He is swinging his body around. Soon he will be able to move forward and backward, and will be walking instead of crawling. You are a very lucky little girl to be able to watch a tiny baby grow. It is one of the most exciting sights in life."

Rachel put her chair down by the playpen, and snuggled her face to the baby's. He grabbed and hung on to a piece of her long blonde hair. Tears came to her eyes.

"Let go, Sunny, let go!"

Baby held tight.

Mother came to the rescue. She gently opened the baby's fist.

"He hurt me, Mother."

"Yes, I know he did. But he did not mean to do so. He saw your pretty soft hair so close and he just grabbed it. He is too little yet to know he is hurting when he does that. It will be up to you to keep your hair out of his way. Soon he will understand 'let go' when you say it. And soon he will have learned how to let go. It is easy for a baby to learn to grab. It is much harder to learn to open up the fist and let go. You were the same way. But you learned to stroke hair gently. You loved to run your fingers through hair. I could even trust you with the cat, for you never pulled her fur."

"Look at him grab his rattle, Mother. He's a strong little man, isn't he?"

"Yes, indeed. He can hold on very tight. But watch, and sometime you will see him even cry because he wants to let go, and hasn't yet learned how. I am writing a lesson for some young children, and I think that today we have learned a lesson from the baby. Can you tell me what it is?"

"Be kind to babies."

"Yes. And what have we learned by watching baby?"

"That babies pull hair."

"Anything else?"

"They don't let go of what they grab."

"How true! Only when we grow up do we really learn how to let go. It is a hard lesson to learn. There is a verse in the Bible about which I have been asked to write: 'Beware of covetousness; for a man's life consisteth not in the abundance of the things which he possesseth.' "

"Are you telling a story in your lesson?"

"Yes, I am."

"Please try it on me."

"I will. And if you don't understand, you tell me. Because then I will know that I am writing to grown-ups and not to you. Once upon a time in the land of India . . ."

"Goody! I love stories about India."

"There lived a little boy. Every Saturday his mother would make the most delicious fried candy for the family. She would cook these candies called jellabies in deep fat, and when they were cooled she would keep them fresh by placing them in a large earthen jar. This was a big jar, but it had a very small mouth.

"One Saturday after she had finished her cooking, the mother went to sweep the front yard, and to clean up after the chickens and other animals which slept in a room near the family. While she was outdoors, her little boy . . ."

"How little?"

"Not so big as you."

"As little as Sunny?"

"A little older than Sunny. Now where was I?"

"While the mommy was outdoors the little boy . . ."

"Oh, yes. The little boy toddled over to the jar and put his hand in and tightened his fist around some delicious candy . . ."

"He shouldn't do that."

"That's right. But he was very small. Perhaps he was too small to know that he was being bad. Anyway he got into trouble. His hand had gone into the jar easily; but now with his fist full of goodies he couldn't pull his hand free. He pulled and he tugged. He started to scream for his mother. He was afraid that forever and ever he would be stuck to the jar."

"Poor little boy. I hope his mother hurries and comes."

"She did. When she saw what had happened she dried his tears and told him what to do. Do you know how she got him loose?"

"She broke the jar."

"No. That would have been a shame. The jar was a good jar. And the family was not rich. Besides the boy's hand could have been hurt if the jar was smashed."

"I can't guess, Mother."

"How did the boy's hand get into the jar?"

"He put it in."

"Then why couldn't he pull it out? What goes in usually comes out."

"He had the candy."

"Yes, he had the candy in his fist. When his hand went in it was open and didn't take up much room. But with a fist he could not back out of the hole. Now can you guess what his mommy told him to do?"

"Let go of the candy."

"That's it! And out came the hand."

"Poor boy! He lost the candy."

"Yes, but would it have been better to have the candy and lose his hand?"

"No."

"Christians have to learn to let go. We are not

to be greedy. We are not to be covetous. And do
you know, my dear, I have a feeling that the boy's
mommy, after she had dried his eyes, reached in
with a forked stick and pulled out a delicious
jellabie for him.

"God, we know, does that for us. Didn't He say
that it was His good pleasure to give you the
kingdom? Lesson is ended. Did you understand
it?"

"I did. May I name it? Let's call it 'Sunny, Let
Go!' " said Rachel.

# Sins of Omission and Commission

"Keep My commandments." John 14:15

"All of my children like big words," said Mother.

"Even if we don't use them right," said Judy.

Mother laughed. It was a family joke. When Judy came to live with the family and adopted them she would often go along when Mother spoke to missionary meetings. The part she loved most about the trips was the wonderful meals some hostess family would feed them. The part she liked next best was the discussion groups—the talking the women did after Mother had finished her speech. On her return from one of these journeys Daddy had asked her if she had enjoyed herself. "Yes, Daddy," Judy glowed with happiness, "especially the ladies when they were disgusting!"

Mother told the children of a mistake she had made when she had been a little girl. One day she had asked her daddy what a "pyonder" was. And her daddy had been puzzled.

"You sing it all the time," she insisted. It had been one of little Edna's favorite songs. She sang it

110

for her daddy: "When the roll is called a pyonder I'll be there."

Daddy laughed at her. "You just glued two words together that don't belong together." Daddy had explained to her that it was not a "pyonder," but "up yonder." "Up yonder" was a phrase that little girls seldom used; even grown-ups would probably say instead of "up yonder," "up over there," for "yonder" meant "over there." It was a way of describing a land by its location. The song-writer was telling the world that "when the roll is called in heaven, I'll be there," Mother's daddy had patiently explained.

Rachel had come to Mother one morning to ask when the bombs were going to start to fall. Mother had been surprised at the question because she could not remember any discussion about war that had been overheard by her little girl. Before she had a chance to answer, Rachel had puzzled her even more by saying she hoped it would be soon.

"Why?" asked Mother. Whenever Mother did not understand a question she had found it best simply to ask "why?"

"Because," Rachel had replied, "I want to go to Pittsburgh soon. And you told me we would go on the first bomby day."

Mother talked a little differently from the rest of the family because she had been brought up in

India, and Rachel had thought she had said "bomby" when what she had said was "balmy." Mother was waiting for a beautiful, warm, and pleasant time for the drive—a balmy day.

But even though the family all made its mistakes, Daddy would say, "It is better to make mistakes and use new words than to wear the old tired words to death." That is why one of their favorite games had two big words in the title. It was the game of "Sins of Omission and Commission." It grew out of the Westminster Shorter Catechism which Daddy knew by heart, but which all the children and Mother had to memorize.

"It is good for all of us to learn it," Mother had said. Mother had not been born a Presbyterian, and so she learned it with the children. "It isn't exactly short," she would sigh, "but it is concise." "Concise" was a favorite word of Mother's. It was the opposite, she would say, of beating about the bush. She did not like to use two words if one would do the job just as well. Being a mother had made her this way. She would explain that if Rachel were about to step off the sidewalk it was much better to call, "Stop." If she said, "Keep your feet on the sidewalk," it would probably be too late. By the time she had the words out, Rachel, as quick as she was, would have reached the other side of the street.

Sometimes the Shorter Catechism used words that were too big for a child Rachel's age. But they did not waste a word, and the family could always figure out what the words meant. This was good for the vocabulary.

The definition it gave for sin was, Mother thought, a beauty in brevity. The question went, "What is sin?" And the answer was, "Sin is any want of conformity unto, or transgression of, the law of God."

"A want of conformity unto," Daddy had explained, was a sin of omission. Then he went on to put that into crayon crowd words: "not doing what God told you to do." "A transgression" was a sin of commission. That meant, in Rachel's vocabulary, "you cut straight across a stop sign of God's." To help them understand it he had made up this game for the family, "Sins of Omission and Commission."

Today with Daddy home they decided to play "Sins of Omission and Commission" after devotions. Mommy sometimes got mixed up on the sins, so she was happy when Daddy played the game with them.

"Rachel, you are the littler, you may go first. Then if you don't know, Judy can help out."

"Count me out," said Mother. "This game is for logicians. I will be the scorekeeper."

"If Mommy tells you, Rachel, to feed Tippy and you don't, what kind of sin is that?"

"Omission, Daddy."

"Good. Now be careful: if Mommy asks you to feed Hamlet and you do—"

"That isn't a sin, Daddy."

"I can't catch you, can I?" said Daddy.

"Keep trying," pleaded Rachel.

"Let me ask Judy a hard one. If I say to Judy, 'Don't wash the dishes,' and she does . . ."

"I wouldn't call that a good example," said Mother.

"Did anyone hear Mother say she wasn't playing?" teased Daddy.

Judy laughed. "That would be a sin of commission."

"Why?"

"Because I disobeyed you. I did what I was told not to do. I cut across a commandment. I transgressed against a commandment of God."

"That is what I call answering a question," said Daddy. "Now anyone may answer these questions. I tell you to go to church and you don't."

"Omission," both girls answered.

"Study your Sunday school lesson and you don't."

"Omission." Judy was the first this time.

"Give us a commission one, Daddy. We have

too many omissions," said Rachel.

"What does that probably show us?" asked Daddy.

"We do more omission sins than commission," said Judy.

"Often we do not even think of omission sins as sins. Transgressions of the law of God, or sins of commission, are easy to spot. But the others are not usually so clear. You try to give me an example of a sin of commission, Judy."

"Pray, and you don't. No, that's a sin of omission."

"I know one, I know one," said Rachel.

"It's sissy's turn," said Daddy.

"Let her go first," said Judy.

"Eat your spinach and you don't."

"Is that a sin of commission?" asked Daddy.

"No, that is omitting to do something you were told to do which makes it a sin of . . ."

"Omission," called Rachel.

"Now let's make that into a sin of commission. You take this, Judy."

"Don't eat your spinach and you do."

"Excellent," said Daddy.

"Can't you find better examples?" asked Mommy.

"Listen to the voice in the bleachers," said Daddy. "Why not give us a good example,

Mother?"

"Do not lie and you do."

"Oh, that gives me an idea," said Judy. "Now I can go through all the commandments."

"First answer Mother's," said Daddy, who never let anyone get off the subject.

"Commission," said Judy. "Now how about, do not hate and we do."

"Commission," said Rachel.

"Rachel, can you think of one of the commandments?" Rachel started to count them on her ten fingers. "I can't think of any."

"We shall have to take time out and review them for Judy and introduce you to them, Rachel."

"Rachel knows most of them," said Mother. "She has just blacked out."

"Give me a hint, Daddy."

"I will try to turn on a light in your blackout. How about cookies and the cookie jar?"

Rachel blushed. "I helped myself and Mommy told me not to eat any cookies before dinner."

"What kind of sin would that be?"

"Commission."

"What commandment would that be that you transgressed?"

"Thou shalt not . . . Help me, sissy."

"Don't help her, sissy," said Mother.

"Steal," shouted Judy.

"What sin was that which Judy just committed?" asked Daddy. "Mother told Judy not to help, and she did."

"Commission, commission," shouted the girls together.

"I don't like that example," frowned Rachel. "Sissy was helping me."

"Which brings up another problem," said Daddy. "Should we ever do something wrong because it is for a good cause?"

"Yes," said Rachel stubbornly. "I want sissy on my side."

"What if Mommy had told Judy to help you and Judy had refused to do so? Judy may have thought it was better for you to think for yourself. What kind of sin would that have been?"

"Omission," said Rachel.

"It is dangerous," said Daddy, "to disobey, to sin, thinking it is for good. 'The end justifies the means,' this kind of thinking is called, and people practicing it can end up in all kinds of serious trouble. People have actually murdered others in order to convert them to God. They have broken the Sixth Commandment for the best reason in the world. We are fortunate that not too many people have gone to this extreme—this far," said Daddy. Daddy was always having to back up to find crayon words.

"By the way, we sidetracked; what commandment was it that Rachel broke when she raided the cookie jar?" Daddy had Rachel hold up her ten fingers and as the family said the commandments he helped her tuck a finger down for each one.

"Thou shalt not steal. I got it. I got it," said Rachel happily. "I broke the—"she counted all the downed fingers—"I broke number eight."

"Never break the law of God for any reason whatsoever. Keep the commandments. If you don't, what sin is that?"

"Omission," chorused the family.

# How to Get to Heaven

"Be ye therefore perfect, even as your Father which
is in heaven is perfect." Matthew 5:48

"Mother," Judy said, "my Sunday school
teacher said that none of us was good enough to
get to heaven if we counted on our own good
works. She said even she wasn't. She was wrong,
wasn't she?"

"Let's test it," suggested Mother.

"Let me play too," called Rachel from the other
room where she was tucking her favorite doll, Betty
Nancy, into her cradle for her afternoon nap. She
joined Mother and Judy in the kitchen where they
were peeling potatoes. Mother made such skinny
peelings. She said it was because she had grown up
on the mission field and had learned not to be
wasteful of food. Judy's peelings always came off
in clumps. But it wasn't that she didn't try. It was
because her fingers hadn't had as much practice.
Rachel wasn't allowed to use a sharp knife as yet.
Even her scissors had round tips. But she could
wash the potatoes when they had them baked.
Maybe that was why baked potato was her favorite
kind.

Now Mother put all the cut-up pieces into the

pressure cooker to make her special "hurry-up stew." She wiped the table and went to her kitchen drawer. Mother had wonderful things in her kitchen drawer—not just kitchen things. She had things to play with on a rainy day, and things for Rachel to do while Mother cooked, and even some rattles for Sunny. The rattles were in the shapes of the ABC's. Rachel knew the alphabet letters backward and forward. Mommy said she was precocious and that if Sunny played with alphabet rattles maybe he would grow up to be precocious too. Rachel did not know what the word meant, but she guessed it meant "precious." It sounded like it. She did not understand why Sunny was not precocious now. She was puzzled and when Rachel was puzzled she would ask questions.

"What does 'precocious' mean, Mommy?"

Mommy did not understand what "precocious" had to do with the kitchen drawer, but she answered Rachel in the way she usually did when she wanted to know the meaning of a word.

"It means the opposite of stupid."

"Now I see," said Rachel.

"See what?" asked Mommy, and then went on with what she was doing before Rachel could answer. She was pulling out of the kitchen drawer two sheets of clean white paper, a ruler, and a black crayon. She had forgotten Rachel had asked a question, and Rachel did not bother her with the answer. She was too interested herself watching what Mommy was doing. She was spreading the two sheets flat on the kitchen table. Then taking the ruler she placed it in the center, parallel to the long edge of one of the sheets. She let Rachel take the crayon and draw a line beside the ruler. It divided the page into two parts. The line squiggled a little but it was mostly in the middle. Rachel did better on the second sheet of paper.

"Now we shall see if Mrs. Henderson, your Sunday school teacher, was right. We are always to test things other people tell us."

"Even you, Mother?" asked Rachel.

"Even me," said Mother.

"Are you ever wrong, Mother?"

"I'll tell you a secret, Rachel. Don't tell anyone. But sometimes I am."

"We won't tell," shouted Rachel. "We won't tell, will we, Judy?"

"This time we are checking on what Mrs. Henderson said. Now, Judy, write your name on the top of this page and you write your name on the top of the other, Rachel."

"Help me, Mother, please."

Mother folded Rachel's fingers about the crayon and Rachel bit her tongue between her teeth hard, but not hard enough to hurt. This always helped her write. It was slow work but at last she had it all written.

"Judy always finishes first."

Judy smiled. "That is because I only have four letters in my name. Let's count how many you have."

"I can only count to ten."

"Maybe there won't be that many. Let's try." Judy pointed to each alphabet letter in "Rachel." Rachel held up a finger for each one.

"Six. There are six. You see," said sissy, "you have to write two more letters than I have to."

"We're done, Mommy," both girls called. "Now what do we do?"

Mother thumbtacked the pages onto the big bulletin board that hung in the kitchen. But first of all she had to take down some of the clippings that were there to make enough room. There were recipes and newspaper articles and poems and cartoons. There were always lots of Marmaduke cartoons. Marmaduke was a newspaper dog that did so many funny things. He was a Great Dane like Hamlet. Mother gave these cartoons to Rachel who was making a scrapbook full of these. The one today showed him coming down the front walk of the house carrying a tiny kitten in his mouth. Mother was waiting for him in the doorway. The words underneath said, "No! You may not have a pet."

After the bulletin board was ready with the new pin-ups, Mother said, "Now we shall see if you girls are good enough to get to heaven on your own good works. Every good thing you do, you come and tell me and I will make a mark on the good side. Every bad thing you do, you come and tell me and we shall put a check mark on the bad side."

"Let's call the columns 'plus' and 'minus,' " suggested Judy. "Then Rachel can tell easier. And could we make our own markings instead of telling you?"

"I can't reach," said Rachel. "I don't mind, Mommy, you can mark mine."

"Fair enough," said Mother.

"How good do we have to be to make heaven?" Rachel asked.

"What does the Bible say?" asked Mother.

Nobody answered.

"Judy, you read Matthew 5:48 for us."

Judy was a good reader. She read carefully and loudly. "Be ye therefore perfect, even as your Father which is in heaven is perfect."

"What does perfect mean?" asked Rachel.

"No mistakes."

"We'll try," said Rachel.

As the day went along Rachel kept running back to Mother to have her write down the good deeds she was doing. When she walked slowly Mother knew it was going to have to be a black mark in the minus column. Judy was filling up both sides of her sheet also, and before bedtime both girls were sad at all the black marks they had scored in the bad column.

"Maybe if you gave us gold stars in the good column that would help," suggested Rachel.

Mother got out the box of gold stars from the kitchen drawer, and the next day, rather than write down what good deeds had been done, Rachel pasted in gold stars while Mommy held her high enough in the air. And only for bad deeds she let Mommy mark with the black crayon. Rachel kept her eye on sissy's sheet too. "Judy's not perfect yet either."

Mother smiled. Every day Rachel kept hoping. Finally on the last day of the week she cried. "I didn't make it, Mommy."

"No," said Mother, "and neither did Judy."

"So Mrs. Henderson was right," said Judy.

"I want to go to heaven," cried Rachel.

"How do we get there, Mother?" asked Judy.

"We should have put another piece of paper on our bulletin board."

"Daddy's?" asked Rachel.

"No, even Daddy would have black marks. The name over this white sheet of paper would be

'Jesus.' Would He have had any black marks by the end of the week?"

"No, only gold stars," said Rachel.

"He was perfect," added Judy.

"That is what Mrs. Henderson was trying to tell you. Our works won't get us to heaven, but Jesus' works will. He lived a perfect life and at death He took all our black marks and put them on His sheet of white paper. He became sin for us."

"He dirtied His paper for us," said Rachel.

"That is exactly what He did. And now God does not see your black marks because Jesus' white paper covers it completely. When God the Father looks at your paper all He sees is a spotless sheet of white paper. It looks as if you had never even been bad. And how welcome you will be in heaven."

Mother took the stew off the stove. It smelled so good. "Kitchens are wonderful places," said Rachel.

Mother started to hum. She often hummed in the kitchen. Rachel would often try to guess what she was humming. Today Mother started to sing the words, "There was no other good enough to pay the price of sin. He only could unlock the gate of heaven and let us in."

# On Priorities

"Seek ye first the kingdom of God." Matthew 6:33

"Mommy, what is a porty?"

"I don't know, darling."

"You wrote a poem about them. 'Porties' you called it."

"Oh! Daddy has been talking. I know now what you mean. The college where Daddy went to school invited women to write poems about how they felt about being women. And Mommy was very honored when they picked the poem she sent in to be published with many others from all kinds of women from all parts of the United States."

"Read it to me, please."

"I don't think you are ready for it yet, honey. Maybe when you are a little older you will understand it."

"Please, Mommy. I don't want to wait until I grow up. You can explain it to me. Let's both sit down and rock while you tell it to me."

"It does help us to think when we rock together, doesn't it? Here is the poem. I call it 'Priorities.' Let me read it first and then let us see if we can figure out why Mommy called it by that funny title."

## *Priorities*

*The sea is wild today. The rough waves unkindly*
*Lap up my sand etchings erasing what I have*
*So laboriously sketched*
*By its shoreline.*

*Tomorrow I shall sit further from the ocean,*
*Draw in the sheltered dunes where my meager talent*
*Will be safe, surviving*
*Its erosion.*

*Nearby my children will be building sandcastles.*
*How shall I shield my art from their bare feet ebbing*
*Surging all about me?*

*And why?*

"What did you think about while I was reading my poem?"

"Ocean City," said Rachel.

"It happened there," smiled Mother. "I was drawing in the sand. What washed away my paintings?"

"A big wave?" asked Rachel.

"The first time, yes."

"I don't like it when the water washes my pictures away."

"Could you see from the poem what else rubs out Mother's paintings?"

"Sometimes Sunny crawls over them."

"Yes, Sunny does. You, honey, of all the children, try very hard not to mess up Mother's sketches in the sand. That is because you are a little sand artist yourself. It takes a poet to understand one. But in the poem I took what is called poetic license; that means I said "children" when I was really thinking of Sunny. I said all of your bare feet. More than one pair of bare feet would make more of a mess, I thought, and explain what I meant better. I could not put in how careful you are, at least not in this poem, because I felt this poem should have just one point, the point of priorities."

"I don't want anything you draw to be spoiled, Mother."

"I shall have to write a poem some day about my sensitive daughter. That means a poem about a little girl who cares very much about her loved ones and does not want to hurt them or have anybody else harm them. Do you know what 'meager' talent means?"

"You like to do it."

"I think you are thinking of 'eager' talent. We both are eager to try to sketch or to write. But 'meager' means that although you try very hard your work is not very good. It is just a little bit good. You know Mother would never have published any books at all if it were not for Daddy. He told Mother one day she was aiming for the moon when she should shoot for a star. He meant Mother had meager talent; but God expects us to develop a ten-talent mind also. In fact, Daddy said that in church work he had found that the Bible story about the talents was so true. People with many talents usually used them to the fullest. The person in the church to ask to do a job is always the busiest. He will do it willingly and well. The person with the meager talent will be too shy and will say 'no' too quickly and run and bury the little bit he has. Do you understand what I am trying to say, Rachel?"

"I understand it, but I don't like it. Mommy, you are the most wonderful poet in the whole wide world."

"Wouldn't it be wonderful for Mommy if all the people in the world were four-year-old Rachels? Thank you, darling. But to get back to priorities, which is more important? Should I let Sunny, our gurgler baby, come gooing and crawling to me even if he blots out my sand picture, or should I push him away and save my sand etching? Is my picture more important than Sunny?"

"No," sighed Rachel. "But I wish he wouldn't

do it."

Mother laughed. "Sometimes *I* wish he would-n't, darling. But now for the word in the title, 'priorities.' Do you understand what it means?"

"It means putting Sunny first and the painting second."

"Correct. We give Sunny priority. Sunny and you and Sissy and Daddy. As a wife and mother you are my first priorities. That is what I was trying to say. Then if I can do something else, that is icing on the cake. Speaking of which, the cake is cool. Which color frosting shall we use?"

"Any kind, so long as it is yellow."

"Yellow," said Mother, "has priority with you. We will make a lemon frosting."

"Is that yellow?"

"Yellower than yellow. Which reminds me," said Mother, "as Christians it is very important that we get our priorities straight. Who should come first with Mother, even before her family?"

"God."

"Let's learn this verse while we frost the cake: 'Seek ye first the kingdom of God.' "

# The Ninety and Nine

"Thy rod and thy staff they comfort me." Psalm 23:4

Rachel's favorite picture in her room was of the Good Shepherd. It showed him leaning over a cliff rescuing a little lost sheep. Her favorite hymn was "The Ninety and Nine." Once in a while instead of following a Bible book for devotional readings Daddy would ask for favorite topics. On her birthday it was Rachel's turn to choose, and everybody knew what it would be. It always surprised Mother that as often as the family had devotions on this subject there was still something new Daddy found in the Scriptures about lost sheep.

This time he had them sing a new song about sheep, one the family had not sung before. It had in it the line, "Prone to wander, Lord, I feel it, prone to leave the God I love."

As always there were words to explain. "What crayon word can we find for 'prone?' " Daddy asked. Judy got out her school dictionary and looked up the meaning of the word.

"It means 'disposed,' " Judy said. Then Daddy asked what "disposed" meant and Judy had to look that word up too. "It says, 'inclined.' "

"And what does that mean?" asked Daddy who

never gave up.

Judy looked up the word "incline." "People who write dictionaries are dumb. Why do they explain a word with another difficult word?"

"What does 'incline' mean?" persisted Daddy.

"To favor," read Judy. She finally knew what "prone" meant. She knew what "favor" meant. She often talked about children in school being favorites, or teacher's pets. It meant they were liked best. "So 'prone' in crayon language means 'likes best,' " she answered.

The next large word was "wander." Rachel had her children's dictionary in front of her. It had the words and then pictures explained their meaning. But Daddy told her that since it would be hard to draw a picture of "wander," she would probably not find it in her dictionary. He told her to look in the "W's." He was right. They could not find "wander" there.

"Do you want to guess, Rachel?"

"Beautiful."

"I think you are thinking of 'wonder,' or 'wonderful,' " said Daddy. "No. 'Wander' does not mean 'beautiful.' "

"Give me a hint, Daddy."

"Sometimes when we take trips I call you the 'Happy Wanderer.' Does that help?"

"I like to go on trips," said Rachel.

"That is what it means, but it means more than that. When I ask you where we shall go, Rachel, you always say, 'Anywhere, Daddy, just so we go.' That is why I call you my 'Happy Wanderer.' When I ask Mother where we shall go, she will say, 'the shopping center or some special restaurant.' She is a happy traveler, but not a happy wanderer. Now what is the difference? I know by the smile on Judy's face that she has guessed it, but since this is your birthday we will let you have first chance at answering all the questions."

"Give me another hint, Daddy."

"You will go anywhere. Mother will go some-where. Does that help?"

"Let Judy answer," said Rachel.

"Judy?"

"Mother has a destination."

"Right. But was my big girl saying something a moment ago about dictionary writers explaining a big word by a bigger one? 'Destination,' to put it into crayon words, means knowing where you are going. A wanderer goes from one place to another with no plan, without thinking. Now to get back to our hymn: 'Prone to wander' means I like very much to go from one place to another with nowhere special in mind.

"Let's say the line again, and think of its mean-ing: 'Prone to wander, Lord, I feel it, prone to leave the God I love.' Now we know what it means. I like best Lord, I feel it, I like best to go from one place to another leaving behind me the God I love. I go to nowhere in particular, and for no reason. We leave, notice the song says, we leave the God we love. It would make sense if we left the God we hated. What kind of sheep are those who wander away?"

"Black sheep."

"Yes. But what would we call the white sheep who love the Lord that also wander away?"

"Silly sheep."

"Let us say the Twenty-third Psalm together and see how the Lord cares for these silly sheep who are 'prone to wander.' "

The family recited it together. Daddy stopped them when they came to the verse, "Thy rod and thy staff they comfort me." He went to his study and brought back with him a shepherd's crook or staff he had bought from a shepherd in Bethlehem. He had Rachel bring down from her bedroom her favorite picture of the Good Shepherd. There the artist showed Jesus using a staff, like the one Daddy had in his hand, to save the lost sheep from falling over the steep cliff and being killed.

"This silly sheep whom God had been feeding on green grass and giving to drink by the quiet waters had been prone to wander, and the Good

Shepherd had left the ninety and nine to find it."
Daddy gently placed the hook of the staff around
Rachel's neck. He held it there. "Now you try to
wander, Rachel." She pulled.

"It hurts, Daddy."

"It won't if you stop pulling," said Daddy. This
crook will keep you in the right path. And if you
stray, the Lord will use it to rescue you as He did
this little lost sheep in the picture. This is the part
of the Twenty-third Psalm I like the best. God will
hurt us if necessary. He loves us enough to use the
crook rather than let us tumble our own way over
the cliff. That is why the psalm says, 'Thy rod and
staff comfort me.' The staff does not frighten, it
comforts. God will use it to save us from the wild
enemies about; He will use it for our protection.
But most wonderfully of all, He will use it on us
for our own good, to keep us from killing ourselves.

"They say in Palestine that sometimes a shepherd, a good shepherd, will break the leg of a sheep
to keep it from wandering away. While the leg is
mending the sheep must limp close to the shepherd, and he is cured from his bad habit of wandering."

"I hope He won't break my leg," said Rachel.

"I hope He won't have to," said Daddy. "You
know, Rachel, your name means 'lamb.' We call
you our lamb. The Bible talks about silly sheep but

it also talks about lambs, the dear ones of God. Do you know whom the Bible calls the Lamb of God?"

"Jesus."

"Yes, Jesus the Good Shepherd is called the Lamb of God. On your next birthday, if you want to wait that long, we will talk about that Lamb of God. But my birthday prayer for tonight and always is that you will not be a silly sheep, but a little lamb of God."

"Amen," said Rachel, looking at her little bare feet. "I don't want Jesus to have to crook me."

# The Lamb of God

"Behold the Lamb of God that taketh away
the sin of the world." John 1:29

"Daddy, I can't wait for the lesson on the Lamb of God," said Rachel, the very next day after her birthday.

"I can't think of a better reason to have it tonight for devotions, can you?" answered Daddy. "So let's get to work. This will be a harder lesson than some. You will have to stop me if you do not understand. I shall start with a question: Why is Jesus called the Lamb of God? And I shall give you the answer. That's an easy start, isn't it? Read the answer for us, Mother, in your Bible. Isaiah 53:7. This is a description of Jesus."

Mother read: "Like a lamb that is led to the slaughter, and like a sheep that is silent before its shearers, so he opened not His mouth."

Daddy continued, "We know that shearers are farmers who raise sheep. The pretty orange sweater that you are wearing, Rachel, is made from wool. The shearers cut the heavy, thick hair from their sheep and sell it at the market. It is twined into wool. Mommy buys the wool and you have seen her knitting it into sweaters for the family. But

137

sheep farmers also slaughter. Judy, do you know what 'slaughter' means?"

"Killed. The sheep are killed in the slaughter-house."

"Oh no!" said Rachel. "Who would kill a lamb?"

Rachel had become a vegetarian the day she learned that meat came from animals. Mother had tried to explain to her that if animals were not slaughtered there would be more animals on the earth than green grass and everybody would starve to death. It would start a chain that would lead to worldwide famine. Animals were put here for man-kind to eat. But Rachel was stubborn. She stayed a vegetarian.

Today Daddy opened up this delicate subject again by telling Rachel it was a quick death in the slaughterhouse. Animals were killed as quickly and as painlessly as possible. He could see this was too sad a subject upon which to dwell with Rachel.

"You may stay a vegetarian, Rachel. So long as Mother gets into you enough of the foods that make you grow. You are my little Danielle. We shall feed you on pulse."

"What's pulse, Daddy?"

"Pea soup."

"I like that. I will be a Danielle," said Rachel.

Whenever it was possible Daddy tried not to

offend the likes and dislikes of the children. There were enough commandments, he would say, that he did not want to be a Pharisee and add to the burdens of the do's and don'ts God had given.

"In the days of the Old Testament, God commanded His people as a part of their worship service to sacrifice an animal in the temple for their sins."

"But why, Daddy? Doesn't God love the animals?"

"Very much," said Daddy. "We had a young friend who went to a foreign field as a missionary for a few years. He said his belief in Christianity was made stronger because of the contrast in the way in which people in this country treated their donkeys. He would see tiny donkeys carrying heavy loads in this heathen land, and then beaten until they got up when they fell to the ground under their hands. God loves animals. The Bible speaks of Jesus tenderly carrying the young lambs in His bosom. But the Bible also speaks of sacrificing lambs. A sacrifice is not a sacrifice unless you give up something that means very much to you."

"Why must God have a sacrifice, Daddy?"

"I will let the Bible answer that question for you. In Hebrews 9:22 we read, 'Without shedding of blood is no remission.' That means no forgiveness. Sin is ugly and horrible. God can't just erase it. For the Bible also tells us the wages of sin is death. Something or somebody must die. There is one story in the Bible that is very difficult for children to understand. Maybe if we think about it a few moments it will help us understand our subject of the Lamb of God. It is the story of Abraham and Isaac. You remember that, to test his faith, God asked Abraham to offer up his only son as a sacrifice."

"When I was a little girl," said Mother, "and I came to a picture of Abraham sacrificing his son Isaac, I asked my daddy who that bad man was."

"Many little girls and many grown-ups feel that way," said Daddy. "But it is only because they do not understand. You see, God had a right to ask Abraham to kill his son. Isaac was already sentenced to death. He was a sinner, and the wages of sin is death in this world and the next. Abraham would not have done wrong even if the story ended with his killing his son. He would have been acting in the place of God the judge. He would have been the executioner. Rachel, you may not understand about executions, but in every government there are jails. Bad people are locked up for the safety of the good people. Those who have proved themselves unfit to live are killed by our government. The law is based on the Bible where we are told it is to be a life for a life. Now the man who does the killing is called the executioner. It is his job. He does what the United States Government tells him to do.

"This is the way it was with Abraham. God was the judge. He was responsible. When Abraham did as God told him to do, and prepared to sacrifice his son, he was doing his job. He was acting as God's executioner. It is the most dramatic story in the Bible showing us that the wages of sin is death. Abraham knew this. He knew that his son was a sinner and deserved to die. He knew that he was a sinner and deserved to die. He knew Sarah was a sinner and deserved to die. God could have told Abraham to execute Sarah, but God chose Isaac for a very good reason. It was, you remember, also a test of faith. For Isaac was a very special child. God had told Abraham that through this son the world would be blessed. Now God asked Abraham to sacrifice him. He could have said to God, 'God, you forgot, this is the child of promise.' Instead he went about obeying God. This was a miracle child. He had been born when both Abraham and Sarah were too old to have a child. Abraham knew this was a miracle-working God. He believed God when He told him he would give birth to this son. He believed now that even if he sacrificed his son, God would bring him back to life again. It would simply take another miracle. I am not guessing at this because we read in Hebrews 11:19 that this is the way Abraham felt. He is called a man of faith because he did not hesitate to obey this dreadful command, 'accounting that God was able to raise him up even from the dead.'

"Abraham was a good man, because he obeyed God. Did he have to kill his own child?"

"No," said Judy.

"Why did he stop?" asked Daddy.

"God gave him another offering in place of Isaac, a ram."

"Now, Rachel, let me ask you a question. Would you rather have Isaac be a sacrifice, or the ram?"

"What is a ram, Daddy?"

"A goat."

"I am not overly fond of goats," said Rachel.

"Well, then, we do not have to face a hard decision," said Daddy, relieved. Rachel could have had difficulty choosing between a little boy and a little lamb. Rachel was not overly fond of boys.

"I am quite sure Abraham would not have had any problem deciding," said Daddy. "Think of how Isaac must have felt. He would have had no trouble understanding the Bible teaching that the wages of sin is death. He would always know it. He would always remember also the mercy of God that provided a sacrifice in his place.

"This is a once-in-a-Bible story," continued Daddy. "God never had to repeat this lesson. Nobody else was ever asked to do it. All of us who read it will never forget it. But let me ask you another question. If Abraham had lived in 1974 and he thought God had appeared to him in a dream and said, 'Sacrifice your son,' what should he as a man of faith have done? Mother, this is a grown-up question, so you take it."

"He should have said, 'Get thee behind me, Satan.' It could not have been the voice of God he heard."

"But why?" said Judy. "Why the difference?"

"In Abraham's day, God spoke face to face with His prophets. But we read in Hebrews 1:1–2, 'God, who in divers manners spake in time past unto the fathers by the prophets, hath in these last days spoken unto us by His Son.' Since Jesus' day God does not speak face to face, but speaks to us through the written Word of God. What is the written Word of God?"

"The Bible," said Judy.

"When the Bible was completed we had within our hands the written voice of God. The Holy Spirit leads us into all truth in the Scriptures, and a voice can never be the voice of God when it goes against the direct teaching of Scripture. We know the Bible says, 'Thou shalt not kill.' If Abraham heard a voice telling him in 1974 to kill his son, he would know it was not the voice of God. Since it was telling him to go directly against the teaching of His holy Word, I said it would probably be the voice of Satan."

"Mother is right," said Daddy. "We do still have the voice of conscience today prompting us. But when we get an idea that we have a direct telephone connection today to heaven and can get answers that are not channeled through the Bible, it can lead us all into trouble. Many wonderful Christian people who love the Lord very dearly have done some wrong deeds because of not understanding this. Rachel, are you still with me?"

"Almost," said Rachel.

"Let's play a game, and see if that helps. What if you thought you heard God's voice tell you that on Sunday instead of going to church with us, you should go on a picnic with Suzy? Would that be God's voice?"

"No."

"Why not?"

"God says we should keep the Sabbath holy."

"And . . ."

"Is there any more?"

"You take it, Judy."

"I am not a prophet. He does not speak directly today."

"Do you understand it better now?"

"Yes, Daddy. It is easy. You keep God's rules and you don't make up any of your own."

"I like the way you put it. I only wish I could get it across as easily to some of the grown-ups in my parish. The other day a lady told me she came to church only every other Sunday. She was very proud and happy. Her husband was not a Christian and she told me God had told her to play golf with him one Sunday, then he would come to church with her the next."

"Will it work?" asked Judy.

"Knowing her husband, I doubt it," said Daddy. "But that is beside the point. We never do what is wrong, even for a good reason. Was this the voice of God she heard?"

"No."

"Once again, Judy, why not?"

"The Bible says to go to church regularly. And God does not speak directly today."

"I am glad I am living today," said Rachel.

"I am too. What would I ever do without you? Our story today had a happy ending. But do you remember a Father who let His Son die as a sacrifice for sin? John 3:16," Daddy whispered to Rachel.

She recited it for them: "For God so loved the world, that He gave His only begotten Son, that whosoever believeth in Him should not perish, but have everlasting life."

"We have our answer. This is why we call Jesus the Lamb of God. He is like that ram that Abraham offered up instead of Isaac. He is offered up in our place. Now we need never die."

"Why don't we still offer up lambs, Daddy?" asked Judy.

"Because we do not need to offer any more sacrifices. Jesus was the spotless Lamb of God. During all the days of the Old Testament animals were offered, but once Jesus died for us as our perfect sacrifice it is no longer necessary—it would be wrong to keep on offering up sacrifices. Remember, on the cross Jesus said, 'It is finished.'

"I know, Rachel, how hard it is for you to accept the idea of a sacrifice. Let me ask you a question. Do you think God would have let His Son die for us if there had been an easier way to save us from eternal death? Would He not have been foolish not to take this other way? God is love, sweetheart, but He is also just. Do you know what 'just' means?"

"No, Daddy."

"I am so glad you are honest, Rachel. The only way to learn is to know when you don't know and to be truthful about it. Maybe this will explain the idea of 'just' or 'justice.' Suppose I told both you and Judy not to eat any cookies before dinner. Judy minded me, but you raided the cookie jar. When I came home, what if I just smiled and said, 'It doesn't matter. Let's forget about it.' It might make you happy, but how would Judy feel?"

"It wouldn't be fair," said Rachel.

"That's exactly what I mean. It wouldn't be just. God is just. He could not wipe away something wicked without the price being paid. He could not just forget about it. You know how upset we have been in our own land when we see someone, as we say, 'getting away with murder.' If God simply blinked at sin and pretended not to see it, we would all be getting away with murder. What kind of God would that be, and what kind of world? A sacrifice was necessary. 'Behold the Lamb of God that taketh away the sin of the world.' "

# The Yellow Rug

"Blessed are they whose sins are covered." Romans 4:7

Mother was reading aloud to Rachel some chapters of the book they were writing together. "My! We sound like a saccharine family," said Mother.

"Is that good?" asked Rachel.

"If it is true, it is. But not if it isn't."

"What is saccharin?"

"It is a sugar substitute. People on diets use it in place of sugar. What I meant was that we sound like such a sugary family."

"Little girls are made of sugar and spice," offered Rachel.

"But what about our little baby boy?" asked Mother.

"Oh! Sunny is a very special boy," Rachel said crossly. "He is not made of frogs and snails and puppy-dog tails. He is sugary too."

"Well, that makes two saccharine members of the family."

"What about you, Mommy?"

"I don't feel very sweet today."

"Let's spread the rug, Mommy."

Mother laughed. It was a family secret. In the

bedroom the rug was wearing out and there was a spot where you could almost see the floor. Daddy wanted Mother to buy a new one, but Mother did not ever want to throw out anything. She said it was because when she was a little girl she had lived in India and she had dressed out of a missionary barrel. Rachel always pictured Mother as a little girl in a barrel. Although Mother tried to tell her she did not dress *in* a barrel, but *out of* a barrel, and that a barrel was the way people in America would pack clothing to send to the missionaries, she liked it better her own way.

"Tell me your barrel story, please," begged Rachel.

"You are my favorite audience," said Mother, and she told it again, the story which had been accepted by the missionary magazine when she was Rachel's age. Her mother had written the true story about her and sent it in to be published. "One day Mother's mother, your grandmother now, saw me kissing some clothes from the missionary barrel, especially a little pink dress, almost new, that someone had sent."

" 'Why are you doing that, Edna Rachel?' her mother had asked.

" 'I would like to kiss the kind people who care enough about us to send the barrel. But since they are far away across the seas and I can't, I am kissing the place that their loving hands touched.' "

"Tell about the sad time too," prompted Rachel, who loved to hear her stories over and over again.

"Well, one day my daddy and mother decided it was time for me to have a new coat that nobody had worn before me. It was the first time I would have anything new. I was starting school and I had to go eight hundred miles away from home all alone to a boarding school. They knew I would be homesick and they thought it would be a happy thing to do for me. It was as if with the new coat I would feel their arms of love about me."

"Like Sunny's sleepy blanket."

"Yes. Since they were too far from the city and the stores, they asked the wife of a missionary who lived in the big city to pick out a coat for me and mail it to my school. The big day arrived. My package came. For weeks I had hardly eaten, waiting for my present. I had been picturing a pretty red coat or a bright blue one, maybe with gold buttons. When the teacher opened the package I nearly cried. The missionary had done the right thing. She had picked out a good coat that would wear and wear—one I would grow into, and a good shade that would not show the dirt. It was dark navy blue with black buttons."

"Poor Mommy," said Rachel.

"You are my favorite audience," said Mother again.

Mother, the family knew, because of the missionary barrel days, would keep things much longer than she should. Daddy would laugh and say, "Let's pamper Mother." That meant letting her have her own way. The big sofa in the living room, when a heavy person sat on it, sank way down and the person almost hit the floor. But the sofa stayed.

"If you take that out I will have to be carried out with it," Mommy would say.

"I give up," said Daddy. So the house was full of sagging furniture and threadbare rugs. Mother simply bought a pretty throw rug or some other fancy rug to cover up most of the problems. But in the bedroom, which was a private room in the house, the rug which was used to cover the almost-hole was brought out only on special occasions when people went through the whole house, and on days like this one when Mother was blue for no good reason at all.

When Mother looked at the rug she forgot all her troubles. She would remember the city in Morocco across the seas, where Daddy had bought it for her. It was a bright orange Berber rug, and she and Daddy had sat and drunk black coffee with the storekeeper who had sold it to them. There had been so many other rugs that would not have shown the dirt as much, but when Daddy saw Mother's face as she looked at the orange rug, he remembered the little girl and the navy blue coat, and he had bought it for her. It was one of Mother's treasures.

Rachel ran now and helped Mother get the rug from the cedar chest, and they placed it over the almost-hole, so it didn't show.

"Are you sweet now, Mother?" asked Rachel.

"Yes, indeed," said Mother, giving her a hug.

"Sweet enough to make some fudge?"

"Sweet enough to bake a cake!" laughed Mother.

"I sometimes think," said Mother, as she sifted the flour, "that that rug is like Jesus. I am so fond of things that should be thrown away. I hang on to them. God looking down must think, 'What a silly woman to live in such a threadbare house.' But He doesn't see the holes. He sees only those beautiful covers which we throw over anything that is worn out. Jesus is the orange Berber rug. In Romans 4:7 we read, 'Blessed are they whose sins are covered.' God does not see my threadbare soul, the holes, the sins that are ugly. He sees only beautiful Jesus, my Lord. That should make me saccharine all day long."

"May I lick the dish?" asked Rachel.

"If you keep a spoonful for me," said Mother.

# On Pride

"Love vaunteth not itself; is not puffed up."
1 Corinthians 13:4

"Mommy, I'm all stuck up," said Rachel. She was pasting pictures in the scrapbook she was making for Daddy to take to a little friend in the hospital.

Mommy wiped her hands. "Hurry before Sissy comes home," Rachel insisted, "or she won't like me."

"Why won't she like you?"

"I heard her say the other day that she hates stuck-up people."

"Let me explain what she meant," said Mommy. Sissy did not mean pasty-fingered little sisters. She meant that some people are proud. I don't know why they call that being 'stuck up.' "

"Let's ask Daddy, he'll know. He knows everything."

Mother smiled at Rachel. "If he heard you say that he might get stuck up!"

Rachel laughed.

"Talking about pride, we should remember that sometimes it is good to be proud. It is good to be proud about good things. God tells us in the Bible that we are to think soberly about ourselves. 'Sober' means 'accurately.' We are not to think too highly of ourselves, and we are not to think too lowly of ourselves. When you have worked hard you should feel pride in your work. When I bake a delicious cake I am justly proud about it. Now the kind of pride Sissy is talking about is when somebody has no reason to be proud, when he struts around bragging about something for which he has done nothing. As I remember the conversation, Judy was talking about a friend. They had had a quarrel. Since it was a private conversation between Sissy and myself—even though you were in the room and did hear it—I don't want to mention names, so let's call Sissy's friend by a make-believe name."

"Let me name her, please, Mommy."

"Okay. You are better at naming people than I am."

"Let's call Sissy's stuck-up friend Irene."

"When Sissy called Irene stuck-up," Mommy smiled at Rachel, "it was because Irene did not want to invite another girl—I need another storybook name."

"Is she a good girl?"

"Yes," said Mommy.

"Let's call her Betty." Rachel's favorite doll's name was Betty Nancy.

"Irene did not want to invite Betty Nancy—"

"No, just Betty."

"Irene did not want to invite Betty to her birthday party because her dresses were always so tattered. Judy was right to call her stuck up. Irene—I almost said her real name—does dress beautifully. Her mother sews all her pretty clothes for her. She has a brand-new sewing machine. And Irene's daddy makes enough money so that her mother can buy pretty material for her dresses. Now Betty—"

"Does she dress out of a missionary barrel?" asked Rachel.

"She reminds me of me," said Mother. "She wears what her older sisters have worn before her and sometimes the clothes are worn out before they reach her. Maybe this is why I feel so kindly toward Betty. I know how it feels to be a little girl always dressed in clothes that do not fit or are out of style. But Betty's mother does the best she can. Betty is always clean. Betty's daddy is dead and her mother has to work hard to earn enough to buy shoes for the family. Irene did nothing to have such beautiful clothes. Betty did nothing to have such worn-out dresses. So neither of the girls has anything to be proud or not proud about.

"I like the way the Rev. Paul Smith of Toronto, in his book on 1 Corinthians 13, compares 'vaunting oneself' and being 'puffed up' to a balloon. Vaunting oneself is the outside. How showy a big balloon is. You know how we felt when we tried to climb on the streetcar on the way home from the circus with our big orange balloon. It is very hard to miss seeing a balloon. It vaunts itself.

"It vaunts itself because it is puffed up inside. A balloon is full of air. You have seen how Sissy's cheeks puff up when she tries to blow air into your balloon.

"Yet one prick of a pin or a pinch and all that is left of the beautiful gay balloon is a messy piece of wrinkled rubber.

"You know, whenever I feel like vaunting myself, getting puffed up and acting like Irene—for we are all Irene in moments of our lives—I prick myself with a Bible verse. Let us learn it as our verse for the day. It is found in 1 Timothy 6:7: 'We brought nothing into the world, and it is certain we can carry nothing out.' "

# Good, Gooder, and Goodest

"For unto whomsoever much is given, of him
shall be much required." Luke 12:48

Rachel always noticed shoes. It was Judy who
told Mother why. "Mom, she is at shoe level."

"I never thought of that," said Mother. "It is
hard to remember how the world looked when I
was only three feet high."

Judy brought her mother a cartoon to put on the
bulletin board. It was of a little boy saying to his
big brother, "You'd be afraid of dogs too, if you
were as low down as I am."

"I'm glad God knows our size," said Mother.
"He told us all to be perfect and that means we are
to be good all the time, but He did know we came
in different sizes. We are in different grades in the
school of life."

"He wants us to get A-plus," said Judy, who
was in school.

"A-plus-plus-plus," said Mother.

"I'm not even in kindergarten," said Rachel.

"God wants you to be perfect even this year
before you start kindergarten. He expects more of
Judy, more even yet of Mother, and most of all in
our family of Daddy. But we are all to get A-plus-

plus on our own level. Too many grown-ups act like four-year-olds, and expect God to give them an A."

"And too many grown-ups expect four-year-olds to act like grown-ups and flunk us when we don't," said Judy.

"True," said Mommy. "They expect more than God. By the way, that reminds me of a question you asked last week about why people expect you to behave better than other children just because your father is a preacher. What do you think about this question, Rachel?"

"Does God expect me to?"

"That is a very good question. That is really what is important. There is a verse in the Bible that will help us. Judy, please read to us Luke 12:48, the middle part of the verse."

"For unto whomsoever much is given, of him shall be much required."

"Has more been given to you as preacher's children than to some of your friends? In our home we all go to church and Sunday school. We have family devotions. We say grace at meals. We pray to God. Think of Mary Ann for a moment." Mary Ann was Judy's friend whom they picked up on the way to Sunday school.

"She doesn't have a preacher for a daddy. She doesn't even have a daddy," said Rachel.

"He became tired of being a daddy and ran away," explained Judy.

"I hope our Daddy doesn't get tired of being a daddy," said Rachel.

"He probably does," said Mother. "I sometimes get tired of being a mother. But neither Daddy nor I will run away. Do you know why? We love you too much to be even tempted, but suppose we were?"

"Because the Bible tells you not to. But didn't anyone tell Mary Ann's daddy not to run away?" questioned Rachel.

"Mary Ann's daddy does not read the Bible," said Judy. "And Mary Ann's mother doesn't believe in going to church once you are grown up."

"We hope some day she will," said Mother. "But now you tell me, should you be better behaved than Mary Ann?"

Nobody answered.

"Judy, read our verse again."

Judy read, "Unto whomsoever much is given, of him shall be much required."

"Aren't we the 'whomsoevers' to whom much has been given? So don't be angry when people tell you that you should behave better because you are preacher's kids. The Bible says you should. But people should not expect Rachel to be as good as Judy, or Judy as me or me as Daddy. Fair enough?"

"Fair enough," said Judy.

"Poor Daddy," said Rachel. "Judy and I have to be good. Mother has to be gooder, and Daddy has to be goodest of all."

# God Never Changes

"Jesus Christ the same yesterday, today and forever."
Hebrews 13:8

Rachel loved to shop at the big supermarket with her mother. She knew her alphabet well enough to be able to run around and find lots of items on the grocery list. One day in her hurry she bumped right into Mrs. Adams. There was a great deal of Mrs. Adams, and when she stood in the middle of the aisle it was hard to miss her.

Rachel said, "Pardon me," the magic words. And Mother, who thought she had not said them loudly enough, added her own "I'm sorry."

Mrs. Adams hugged Rachel. Rachel always felt that when Mrs. Adams hugged her she would just disappear into the folds of Mrs. Adams. Still it was better than being hugged by skinny people. Bones hurt. Rachel was a very private person and she would rather not be hugged by strangers at all. But this day she felt she owed it to Mrs. Adams. She hoped the lady's tummy would not be black and blue where she had butted her head into her. She didn't hurt at all. It had been like hitting a soft balloon, and everyone said Rachel was hard-headed. After some talk with Mother, while all the shopping people curved around them like water around a rock, it was time to push their carts in different directions. Just before she left Mrs. Adams said to Rachel, "And how is your Daddy?"

Rachel did not answer right away. Mother said, "Mrs. Adams asked you a question, dear." Rachel was often in a dream world of her own and did not always hear when grown-ups asked questions. Usually Rachel felt, she did not need to answer. It was either "How old are you?" or "What year are you in school?" and if she waited Mother always rushed in to explain that Rachel was big for her age and had not started school. But this time Rachel had heard the question. She was thinking. Now she had the answer.

"He's nice," said Rachel.

Mrs. Adams laughed and laughed. Rachel liked her laugh. Mrs. Adams laughed from her toes. Rachel could hear the laughter rumble way down on her level, but she did not know what she had said that was funny. Mother had to explain that when grown-ups asked how people were they left out an important word. They meant "How is your daddy feeling?" They did not want to hear what kind of person Daddy was. Usually the answer they expected was "Fine, thank you."

"You are absolutely right, honey," said Mrs. Adams. "He is nice." This time Rachel understood. She loved a joke, and she and Mrs. Adams both laughed and laughed.

On the way home Mother talked some more about what Rachel had said. "That was a lovely thing to say about your daddy, especially when you had to think of an answer so quickly. Do you know what 'nice' means?"

"It means 'wonderful,' but I thought I would use a crayon word."

"I thought that was what you meant. There was a time, Rachel, when 'nice' had a different meaning. It was a word you used for 'precise, exact.' Let me see if I can explain what I mean since I cannot find a crayon word for 'precise.' If I told you to cut your paper dolls nicely, it would mean right on the lines, with no cutting off a part of the leg or an arm. I think 'nice' describes your daddy this way too. He wants very much to be a nice person and doesn't want us to be sloppy Christians either. Mother calls him her bundle of consistencies. Now that is a giant of a word. It means he wants us to be nice-good all the time, not one way one day and one way another. He feels we should never take a vacation from being nice-good. People talk about a bundle of inconsistencies. When you put 'in-' in front of a word, it becomes the opposite. You never know what an inconsistent person will do or think. You cannot count on them. Daddy is my bundle of consistencies. Who is the most consistent person of all?"

"God," said Rachel. "Mother, that's easy. When you ask a question, most of the time the answer is God."

"You are right. Just the same, listen carefully to my questions. I may throw you a curve some time." Rachel knew what that meant. She was used to Mother watching baseball on television while she played with her dolls. It meant the pitcher threw the ball in a way that fooled the batter, and it often made the batter miss the ball.

"God never changes," said Mother. "So you can always count on Him. He will never be angry one day over something and not angry the next day over the very same thing."

"God doesn't get headaches," said Rachel.

Mother laughed. "How right you are. One little girl asked her mother, 'Why is it that when I am naughty I am bad, but when you are naughty you have a headache?' "

"Could we play a game about words, Mother?" Rachel always wanted to learn by playing games.

"Yes, let's," said Mother, "but first let's treat ourselves to the long way home so that we can bathe our souls in beauty." They took the mountain road that wound up and down through the thick forest. Mother had to drive slowly. It gave them time to see the view. The leaves on the trees had not yet started to fall. They made a beautiful patchwork quilt of gay colors—the orange of the oaks, the red of the dogwood, the bright yellow of the sugar maples. Rachel and Mother were very much alike. They both liked to be quiet when they saw beautiful sights. No words could be as pretty as an autumn leaf. It was better sometimes to feel and not to try to say how one felt. But after they had passed through what Rachel called her tunnel of trees they started to play the new game.

Mother called it the "in" game. She explained how by putting "in-" in front of a word one could turn its meaning right around, and have it mean the opposite. They had already had an example in 'consistent' and 'inconsistent.' "Try this word," said Mother: " 'considerate.' That means always putting others first."

"Inconsiderate."

"So 'inconsiderate' would mean putting yourself first."

"Lets try the word 'finite.' That is a grown-up word meaning 'with a beginning and an end.' "

"Infinite."

"What would 'infinite' mean, Rachel? It would be the opposite of 'finite.' "

"No beginning and no end."

"Good. Can you think of somebody this word 'infinite' would describe?"

"God. You see, Mother, again the answer is God."

Mother was silent for a long time.

"What's the trouble, Mother?"

"I am having trouble today finding crayon words to fit into our game. How about adding to it by telling you that there are some words that can be changed the same way to the opposite but by adding 'un-' to them. 'In-' and 'un-' in front both turn the word around. Try 'happy.' "

"Inhappy. No. Unhappy."

"Good. Now you will have to watch whether you should use an 'in-' or an 'un-.' "

"Kind."

"Unkind."

"Sad."

"Unsad. No. Insad."

"No," said Mother. "That was a curve question. The opposite of 'sad' is a different word altogether. What are you when you are not sad?"

"Happy."

"Now take the word 'happy,' again."

"Unhappy."

" 'Unhappy' and 'sad' mean the same thing. Isn't it wonderful that we have different words that we can use to get our ideas across? We would get so tired of using the same words over and over again."

"The words would get tired too," said Rachel.

"We have time for one more: 'consistent.' "

"Inconsistent. That's where we started."

"Yes, and that's where we will finish for we are almost to our driveway, and I want to give you a Bible verse to learn which tells us how our wonderful Lord is consistent. In Hebrews 13:8 we read, 'Jesus Christ the same yesterday, today, and forever.' "

Rachel was a quick learner and she knew the verse by heart before they reached the front door.

"Mommy, Jesus Christ is nice, isn't He?"

"Indeed He is," said Mommy.

# If I Should Die

"Yea, though I walk through the valley of the shadow of
death, I will fear no evil; for Thou art with me."
Psalm 23:4


Now I lay me down to sleep,
I pray Thee, Lord, Thy child to keep.
If I should die before I wake,
I pray Thee, Lord, my soul to take.


Rachel knelt beside her bed and said her evening
prayer. This evening when she had finished, she
crawled up into her mother's lap for her good-night
kiss and asked a question.

"Mommy, what does 'die' mean?"

"It means to stop living on this earth."

Rachel knew about this earth. She was very
interested in geography. She knew about Europe
across the water. She knew about missionaries in
Asia. And she knew that although these places
were far away, still they were on this earth. So she
was puzzled.

"Where do you live then when you die,
Mother?"

"If you are God's child you go to live with Him
in His home in heaven. If you are the devil's child

you go to live with him in his home in hell."

"Hell isn't a very comfortable place, is it, Mother?"

"No, it is a *dreadful* place. But remember, dear, only dreadful people go there. Only people who hate God and do not accept God's gift, His Son Jesus, as their Savior."

"I love God, Mother."

"I am glad you do, my darling. I hope all our children love God and believe in Jesus, His Son, who died for His children. That is the dearest wish of my heart. I want you to be happy, healthy, pretty. But most of all I want to know that you are a child of God. Mother and Daddy can't make you a child of God. You are our child, whether you want to be or not. But you must choose to belong to the family of God. If you are His child, then dying means moving to be with Him in His home in heaven. It is a happy time."

"Then why did you cry, Mommy, when Grandfather died?"

"I did not cry for him, darling, because I know he is happier than he ever was in his home here on earth. But I cried because we would not see him on earth again. We could no longer visit him the way we used to do. As long as he was alive, even though he lived a long drive away, we could always go in the car to see him. But now the distance is too great. And we must wait until we die to see him again."

"Will you go with me when I go to heaven, Mommy?"

"No, dear, this is one trip each person must take alone. But it may help if you think of the end of the journey. Let's think of it this way. You know that at Christmas time we used to visit Santa Claus in the department store. The only trouble is that he is on the seventh floor, and we can't walk up that far. How do we go?"

Rachel started to shudder and grabbed Mother's hand. "In the elevator."

"And what is the trouble?" asked Mother.

"I'm afraid of elevators."

"I don't like them either," said Mother. "But it's good to face our fears. This is the first step to overcoming them. You used to call elevators 'alligators,' honey. You seemed to feel they would swallow you up. But remember, you felt it was worth the fright because when you reached the seventh floor the elevator doors opened and there was Santa Claus and all the sparkling Christmas lights.

"Well, darling, death is like the elevator. Nobody really wants to go into the elevator, or die. But although Mommy can't die with you, Jesus goes right along and holds you in His arms. The trip is soon over and when the doors open, there is heaven with its beautiful streets of gold, its gates of pearl. You will see Jesus, your Savior, and Daniel, your favorite Bible person. You will see Grandpa and Grandmother. Everybody will be there whom you have loved who has died as a child of Jesus. And once you are in heaven you will enjoy getting ready for other friends to join you there."

"When will I die, Mother?"

"I don't know, darling. Mother may die first. You may die first. The important thing is to become a child of God. Whoever dies first, then, will be waiting there for the other."

"Mommy, may I say my prayer again tonight?"

"Of course, darling."

Rachel knelt down again beside her bed.

"Now I lay me down to sleep,
I pray Thee, Lord, Thy child to keep.
If I should die before I wake,
I pray Thee, Lord, my soul to take.

"In Jesus name, Amen."

"Thank you for explaining my prayer to me," said Rachel.

# My Moon

"I am come a light into the world." John 12:46

It was Rachel's first night ride. She was thrilled with the big moon shing down on the front lawn. Daddy started the car and they drove out of their own yard onto the highway, past the neighbor's farm and into new country. Rachel, sitting very still, finally could keep her joy to herself no longer.

"Look, Daddy, look!" she called out, pointing to the moon. "It's coming along with us."

Daddy smiled. "Yes, the moon doesn't shine only in our own yard, Rachel. It shines everywhere. It shines on Suzy's lawn—even on the grass huts and wigwams of places far, far away. It is your moon. It is Suzy's moon. It is everybody's moon.

"Did you know," Daddy asked, "that there are many verses in the Bible which speak of Christ as the light of the world. It was said about Him in Matthew 4:16: 'The people which sat in darkness saw great light.' He said of Himself in John 12:46: 'I am come a light into the world, that whosoever believeth on Me should not abide in darkness.'

"He, too, can be seen by all. And, my darling, like the moon He, too, cannot be left behind in our own backyard. He comes right along with us."

# Why Not?

"Work out your own salvation . . . for it is God that
worketh in you." Philippians 2:12–13

"Mommy, what's a robot?"

"A robot, dear, is a doll on strings. A person
pulls the strings and the doll's arms and legs move.
They do not move unless someone outside pulls
the strings. What made you ask, Rachel?"

"Nancy said that I was a robot."

"Why?"

"Because I am a Presbyterian."

Mommy smiled. "I think I know what she
meant. At one time I was not a Presbyterian, and I
thought that if I became a Presbyterian, I could not
move my own arms and legs because God was
pulling the strings."

"Isn't He, Mommy?"

"Yes, He is, dear, in a way. We could do
nothing unless He planned it. But it doesn't mean
that I can't move my own arms and legs."

"What changed you, Mommy?"

"That is an easy question, darling. It was
Daddy. I kept saying to him, 'God can't plan
everything and still let me have my own
freedom.' "

"What did he say?"

"You know Daddy. He never wastes words. He simply said, 'Why not?' "

"What did you say?"

"I just repeated, 'God can't plan everything and still let me have my own way.' "

"And what did Daddy say?"

"He just said, 'Why not?' For ten years that went on. He said a little more. He said, 'Why can't God plan or predestinate (that's just a big word for 'plan') and you still have your freedom? You are not a robot. The Westminster Shorter Catechism says in chapter 10 that God works on people *effectually drawing them to Jesus Christ, yet so as they come most freely.* Why cannot God, who can do everything, predestinate *through* free will—not *against* free will?' "

"What did you say?"

"I kept mumbling, 'He can't.' Then one night I woke up and thought, 'John is right. Why can't He?' And ever since then I have believed in Presbyterianism! I must admit a friend told me a story that helped."

"I love stories, Mommy."

"So do I. This is one that helped me. Mrs. Jones wanted her son Timothy to go to the grocery store with her to help carry the heavy groceries. Now Timothy wanted to go to the grocery store to buy some popcorn. They both wanted to go to the grocery store. Timothy's mother didn't force him to go to the grocery store. She worked through his own wishes. She worked *through* his free will, not *against* his free will. Remember, that is how God works; as our catechism says, 'they come most freely.'

"Just remember, darling, when Nancy calls you a robot, the two words Daddy kept repeating to me. What were they?"

" 'Why not?' "

"Yes, indeed, why not?"

# Red and Yellow, Black and White

"Ye have not chosen Me, but I have chosen you."
John 15:16

Rachel had a lovely voice, a high child soprano, and she sang her favorite song lustily.

*Jesus loves the little children,*
*All the children of the world;*
*Red and yellow, black and white,*
*They are precious in His sight,*
*Jesus loves the little children of the world.*

"Mommy, I have a question," she added at the end of her little song, but Mommy's mind was not listening to her. She was "preoccupied." Rachel loved big words. She loved rolling the word "preoccupied" on her tongue. But this time she did not use her long words correctly.

"Mommy, are you preoccupied?" she said, trying to get her attention. No answer. "Mommy." Mommy still kept on working. Finally, she called, "Edna." That always did it. Mommy jumped.

"Yes, dear, what is it?"

"I want to ask a question. Are you hearing me?"

"Yes," said Mommy, turning off the iron, and she sat down and took Rachel on her lap.

"Does God love Suzy as much as me?" asked Rachel.

"Sing your song again. It says, 'Red and yellow, black and white . . . all the children of the world.' What does 'all' mean, if not each and every one?"

Rachel looked troubled. "What about naughty Mabel, Mother?"

"You have to realize, dear, that love can be used in two ways. There is what we call, dear, a love of benevolence—that's a new word—and a love of complacency. Now, He loves red and yellow, black and white—He loves them all with a love of benevolence. That means, dear, that He is kind and loving to all of them. But is He pleased with the way they all behave? What about Mabel? He loves Mabel with a love of benevolence. But as for the other kind of love, I don't believe from what you tell me that He has that for Mabel. I know she shocked you the other day when she said, 'I hate God. He didn't let me get my way. It rained and I didn't get outside to play.' "

"Does Mabel love God?"

"We can't look into a person's heart, Rachel. We can only see how they act and judge from that. We can make mistakes. Mabel may love Jesus, but it certainly doesn't sound like it, does it? Let us pray for her, and always remember that if she doesn't love Jesus now, she may some day. Do you remember one day, Rachel, when you did not love Jesus?"

"No, Mommy."

"You may not. It may surprise you to know that there was a day when you did not love Jesus. We are not born, honey, loving Jesus. We are all born hating Jesus."

"How sad."

"Yes, it is. We all hate God until a wonderful thing happens. He puts a new heart into us. And now we love Him. We can't have Him close enough."

"Did He put a new heart in me, Mommy?"

"That is something only you and God know. Mommy can only guess by the way you behave, and I feel you act as if He did."

"Why did He not put a new heart in Mabel, Mommy?"

"I don't know why, darling. God could have. He can do anything He wants. He may have, or He may do so some day."

"I want Him to, Mommy."

"Let's pray He will. But remember how we always end our prayers."

"If it be Thy will," said Rachel. "You mean it

may not be His will, Mommy?"

"No, it may not. Darling, you are not too little to think. Who was the very first person that God made?"

"Adam."

"What did he do?"

"He ate of the forbidden fruit. God had told him not to do it."

"Yes, he disobeyed, and that was the very first sin."

"Why did he do it, Mommy?"

"That, honey, is the most difficult question anyone can answer. You are asking it already at age five."

"What is the answer, Mommy?"

"I don't know. Nobody knows. But we do know what God could have done. Ever since Adam we are born not little angels but little devils. We hate God until He changes us. He puts a new heart into us, and now we can never really say we hate God; we can say it in haste and anger, but never really meaning it again.

"That is the new birth. And now we no longer hate God. We love Him. We still do bad things. We pray, you remember, 'forgive us our debts.' But we never again say, 'I hate you, God.' Remember, we can say it in anger (though we must repent), but we never really mean it."

"Why, Mommy, did not God put a new heart in everyone?"

"I don't know, darling.

"I wish you did, Mommy."

"I do too. But remember, God could have done three things after Adam sinned. He could have put a new heart in everyone; or He could have put a new heart in no one; or He could have put a new heart in some. And He chose to change some. Why did He do that, Rachel? Why did He choose to save some?"

"I don't know, Mommy."

"Neither do I, darling. But what do we know about God? What about Him? Does He ever make mistakes?"

"No."

"So whatever He has done is wise. Some day, dearie, we'll understand why He did it. But meanwhile, remember what we always say in our prayers. How do we end our prayers, again?"

"If it be Thy will."

"He, for some reason, known only to Him, chose to save some, not all—not none, but some."

"I'm so glad, Mommy, that He decided to save some."

"So am I, honey. And, remember that we should be grateful to God everlastingly that He chose to change us.

"I'd like to tell you a little story, dear, about a little friend of mine whose name is Michelle. Her daddy had been telling her when she was a little girl that he couldn't even be sure that she was one of those whose heart God had changed, and so he was very careful that she didn't pray to God or think she was a little angel until she really was a little saint. One day a friend of theirs asked the little girl about being a Christian and said to her, "Michelle, you're so sweet. I'll bet you just love Jesus, don't you?'

" 'Not yet,' " said little Michelle, who had been well taught. She wasn't sure herself that she truly loved the Lord Jesus. She had to stop and think, and she thought she did not yet love Him.

"And the most wonderful thing happened, dearie. That little girl some time later—and it wasn't in a month or two, but some time later—came to her mommy and her daddy and said, 'Mommy, I know now I love Jesus, and He has changed my heart.' What a happy day that was for all the family, because now they knew that the Lord had changed her heart, and she was now a little saint. Now she may still sin, but she knew one thing: all of her sins would be covered by the blood of Jesus, because she loved Jesus and repented of her sins.

"That first part of the story was rather sad.

Imagine how the mommy felt when she heard that her little girl had said 'Not yet' when the friend asked her if she was a little Christian. But it was honest. It is much better to be honest than to make a mistake. Sometimes children, to please their parents will say something which is not true. They will say, 'I love Jesus,' when they really don't. How wonderful that the whole family knew that the dear Lord Jesus loved little Michelle, not only with a love of benevolence, but with a love of—what, Rachel? Do you remember what the word was?"

"Complacency."

"Yes. Let's remember this, dear, as we sing the song: that God loves people with two different kinds of love. And let's each one pray in our hearts, 'Come into my heart, Lord Jesus. I want to be loved with the love of complacency.' Here's our little song. Let's sing it together."

*Jesus loves the little children,*
*All the children of the world.*
*Red and yellow, black and white,*
*They are precious in His sight.*
*Jesus loves the little children of the world.*

*Jesus loves the little children,*
*All the children of the world.*
*Red and yellow, black and white,*
*They are precious in His sight.*
*Jesus loves the little children of the world.*

# Other Books for Children
## Published by Soli Deo Gloria

**John Angell James**
*Female Piety*
*Addresses to Young Men*

**James Janeway/Cotton Mather**
*A Token for Children* bound with
*A Token for the Children of New England*

**J. G. Pike**
*Persuasives to Early Piety*
*A Guide for Young Disciples*

**J. C. Ryle**
*Boys and Girls Playing*

**Charles Haddon Spurgeon**
*A Good Start*

For a complete listing of titles, write or call:

Soli Deo Gloria
P.O. Box 451
Morgan, PA 15064
(412) 221-1901/FAX 221-1902